Dorothy Day
for Armchair Theologians

Also Available in the Armchair Theologians Series

Dorothy Day
for Armchair Theologians

ELIZABETH HINSON-HASTY

ILLUSTRATIONS BY RON HILL

WESTMINSTER
JOHN KNOX PRESS
LOUISVILLE · KENTUCKY

© 2014 Elizabeth L. Hinson-Hasty
Illustrations © 2014 Ron Hill

First edition
Published by Westminster John Knox Press
Louisville, Kentucky

14 15 16 17 18 19 20 21 22 23—10 9 8 7 6 5 4 3 2 1

Book design by Sharon Adams
Cover design by Jennifer K. Cox
Cover illustration: Ron Hill

Library of Congress Cataloging-in-Publication Data

Hinson-Hasty, Elizabeth L.
  Dorothy Day for armchair theologians / Elizabeth Hinson-Hasty. — First edition.
    pages cm. — (Armchair theologians series)
  Includes index.
  ISBN 978-0-664-23685-4 (alk. paper)
  1. Day, Dorothy, 1897-1980. 2. Catholic Worker Movement— History. 3. Christian sociology—Catholic Church—History of doctrines—20th century. 4. Radicalism—Religious aspects—Catholic Church—History—20th century. 5. Women social reformers—United States. 6. Catholic Church—United States—History—20th century. 7. Radicalism—United States—History—20th century. I. Title.
  BX4705.D283H56 2014
  267'.182092—dc23
                                                    2014004503

Most Westminster John Knox Press books are available at special quantity discounts when purchased in bulk by corporations, organizations, and special-interest groups. For more information, please e-mail SpecialSales@wjkbooks.com.

For all those who remain unnamed.

Contents

Acknowledgments

This book on Dorothy Day emerged from a larger fascination that I have with expressions of social gospel theology and Christian socialism in the twentieth century, ecumenical collaboration on issues of social and economic justice, and women's involvement in advocacy for people living in poverty. As with all projects of this nature, seldom are they truly written by a single author. They involve the support of a community. That being said, there are quite a few people whom I should thank for their support, sound advice, and encouragement while I was in the process of conducting the research for and writing this book.

I am indebted to the editors and staff at Westminster John Knox Press (WJK). Donald McKim, executive editor at WJK when I undertook this project for the Armchair Theologians Series, encouraged me to reflect on Dorothy Day out of my own experience as a Reformed theologian teaching at a Roman Catholic university. I am grateful for that challenge and how it has encouraged me to grow in my appreciation for both Protestant and Catholic traditions. David Dobson, vice president and executive director at WJK, offered sound advice throughout the process, and Robert Ratcliff, executive editor at WJK, provided valuable feedback and wise suggestions to improve the book's accessibility.

Around the time that I took on this writing project, the Thomas Merton Center at Bellarmine University received a special gift from Mary Alice Zarrella, life partner of Joseph

Zarrella. Joseph Zarrella worked with Dorothy Day in the early days of the Catholic Worker Movement and later established a Catholic Worker house of hospitality in Tell City, Indiana. This gift meant that Bellarmine held nearly a complete collection of Catholic Worker newspapers from 1933 through the 1990s along with some other items. Paul Pearson, director and archivist of the Merton Center, and Mark C. Meade, assistant director of the Merton Center, were both very helpful in accessing the collection and entering into conversation about commitments shared by Thomas Merton and Dorothy Day.

Bellarmine University supported me in this work in numerous other ways. I could not have completed this book without the capable assistance of John Boyd, reference librarian at Bellarmine. The university awarded me a summer research grant in 2005 so that I could travel to Milwaukee to visit the Dorothy Day archives at Marquette University. Philip Runkel, the archivist for the Dorothy Day Catholic Worker Collection at the Raynor Memorial Library of Marquette University, was extraordinarily helpful during my visit there, and I continue to be grateful for his dedication to Dorothy Day and for his precision in cataloging her materials. In addition, Bellarmine generously allowed me to allot part of my sabbatical leave in 2010 to continue my research and reflection on Dorothy Day despite the fact that this project was not intended primarily for an academic audience.

Over the last few years I have tried to visit as many Catholic Worker houses as possible. On several occasions I have taken my classes to the Casa Latina in Louisville, Kentucky, to hear stories told by the "core group" of Workers and people living in the house. I took time to visit other houses when I traveled for meetings throughout the year. Maryhouse in New York City and The Open Door Community in Atlanta, Georgia, figured prominently in my study of Day. I am thankful for both the challenge and the hospitality I encountered in each one of those houses. In addition, I consulted with several Catholic Workers and some of Day's friends and family members either in person, via email, on the phone, or by Skype, including Martha Hennessy, Tom Cornell, Jim Forest, Ed Loring, and Murphy Davis. Their comments and observations were immensely helpful, and I took great delight in speaking with and learning from family members and friends of Day.

There were also many colleagues, friends, and family members who offered their assistance to clarify specific details and read drafts of chapters, supported my time away from the responsibilities of teaching during my sabbatical, and endured enthusiastic (but overly lengthy) conversations about Day as I was reading her with fresh eyes. E. Glenn Hinson, G. Lee Hinson-Hasty, Clyde Crews, Jack Ford, Greg Hillis, Justin Klassen, Isaac McDaniel, Laura Stivers, and Melanie-Prejean Sullivan were all wonderful conversation partners who shared my curiosity about Day's life. Most important, I should reserve special thanks for my colleague and friend Joseph Milburn Thompson, who expressed his own delight that I would take on a project about Dorothy Day, read several chapters with care, and offered graciously his own expertise as a moral theologian.

INTRODUCTION

You may be surprised as you pick up this book that a religious activist and social mystic like Dorothy Day would be the first female theologian included in the *Armchair Theologian Series*. Highbrow academic theologians seldom include Day among the most significant theological thinkers of the twentieth century. After all, Day received no formal theological training in a seminary, divinity school, or university setting. However, there is something distinct about Day's work as a writer and religious social activist.

Day's theological training came from her experiences. She immersed herself in some of the most radical movements for social reform in her day. She discovered her vocation sitting at tables with the hungry, the mentally ill, and the homeless and serving time with people in prison. She sustained her commitments through spiritual disciplines, felt inspired by the liturgical movement, and took regular retreats. She stood on the picket line with the disenfranchised, the unemployed, and the peacemakers and listened to, read, and sought the wisdom of social mystics from the past and those who were among her contemporaries. Most important, Day's schools of theology were houses of hospitality and farming communes of the Catholic Worker Movement. In fact, Day held no academic credentials beyond a high school education. Theologian Philip Kennedy says, "Day lances the boil of the centuries-long conceit that theology is the preserve of monastic, priestly or professorial men."[1]

Day may not have studied at the feet of learned theologians or written books aimed toward an academic audience, but she did author six books during her lifetime and approximately 1,500 articles, essays, and reviews in the *Catholic Worker* paper as well as in other papers and journals such as the *Call*, the *Masses*, *Commonweal*, and *America*. Even without degrees earned from prestigious theological institutions, Day's story, thought, and work captures our attention and enlivens our own theological imaginations.

Dorothy Day was more than an "armchair" theologian enjoying casual conversations about theology with friends from the comfort of her easy chair. She was a theologian with "street cred." Day commands respect because of her experience living among, with, and *as* the marginalized. Her awareness and knowledge of the challenges faced by people living in poverty stemmed from and were shaped by her relationships with them. The presumed distance of academic objectivity does not apply to her story. She did more than think and talk about her faith; she *embodied* it. She did more than challenge the failures of the Christian church or surrounding local community to address the needs of people in poverty; she *created* new community.

Her work also attracted many followers. Women and men dropped what they were doing in their own cities to visit or live at a house of hospitality for a brief period of time or started houses of hospitality in their own areas. Some committed themselves to Catholic Worker communities for much longer periods of time. You may recognize the names of some of the people with whom she collaborated either at Catholic Worker houses or as part of broader social movements—peace activists Philip and Daniel Berrigan, Tom Cornell, Eileen Egan, Jim Forest, Ammon Hennacy, and Thomas Merton; artists Joan Baez, Ade Bethune, and Fritz Eichenberg; civil rights activists and founders of Koinonia farms, Clarence and Florence Jordan; farm worker advocate Cesar Chavez; Pulitzer Prize-winning author and Harvard psychiatrist Robert Coles; and activist, author, and editor Robert Ellsberg. Day also captured the attention of the media and popular culture. The *New Yorker*, the *New Republic*, *Life*, *Time*, and *Newsweek* featured articles on Day's work. She was interviewed by popular talk show hosts such as Mike Wallace and Bill Moyers. Many Catholics remember her as the radical conscience of the American Catholic Church.

In 2000, the Roman Catholic Church initiated the canonization process for her to be declared a saint. For Catholics, this is no small step taken to honor someone's life and work. To be declared a saint by the Roman Catholic Church, one's life must be marked by heroic virtue. The process of canonization has four stages. As I was in the process of writing this book, Day was considered a "Servant of God." The concept of "sainthood" bears different meanings for religious people. Feminist theologian Elizabeth Johnson writes about saints as part of a larger community of "friends of God and prophets."[2] Saints are not human superheroes, but they are models of Christian discipleship. Sainthood is every person's call to truth, love, and holiness.

The title "Saint Dorothy" is one that Day herself resisted. Her famous quote is frequently referenced: "Don't call me a saint. I don't want to be dismissed so easily." This quote certainly reflects Day's resistance to the stories of saints that have been sterilized and sanitized and presented within the tradition as extraordinary models of holiness distanced from the realities of ordinary people. She believed that saints were ordinary people. We each have a vocation and something to give; all that we need to do is just answer that call.

Day certainly did not size up well to traditional models of Christian perfection. She always felt some inner turmoil as a result of some of the choices she made in her youth and fell short of the expectations she had for herself or that others had for her on many occasions. I would not want to make any attempt to sanitize and sterilize her story. The beauty of her story lies in her humanness. Despite her human shortcomings, frailties, mistakes, doubts, and imperfections, she was unable to suppress that gnawing sense of compassion and justice that connects us with others, and she lived out her convictions in communion with God, people, and the planet earth. Her accomplishments will not allow us to dismiss or deny the fact that Day is a model for what it means to be a "friend and prophet" of God.

There is so much that we can learn from Dorothy Day that is relevant for our time. It is not my intention in the pages that follow to systematize her theology, chronicle everything that she did, and name all of the people with whom she worked. That would be an impossible task and go far beyond the scope of this book. I will underline the influence of significant philosophers, theologians, and writers on her thought, but if you as a reader approach my study of Day primarily from a historical perspective or as you would an intellectual biography you will surely be disappointed. To be honest, I fear that Day herself would be disappointed as well if we remembered her work only as a conversation with philosophical and theological abstractions or for the sake of historical study alone. She maintained a lifelong commitment to learning and a searching intellect because she wanted to sharpen her own focus on the world's concerns. My intention is to secure a place for Day among better-known theologians in the history of the church and to consider her relevance for Christians today as we face so many similar economic, social, and political problems.

The first chapter, "Growing to See the World in a New Way," explores the people, places, events, and social movements that made a profound impact on Day's intellectual and spiritual formation. Early on in her life, Day was actively involved in some of the most radical movements for social reform in her time. Her experiences remained with her even after her conversion to Roman Catholicism. Chapter 1 considers how her early life prepared her to walk a lifelong path of resistance as she matured into adulthood and enabled her to see the world and her own role in it in a new way.

Chapter 2, "Synergy," focuses on Peter Maurin, a French peasant who profoundly influenced Day's own thinking and formation. Dorothy met Peter at a critical juncture in her life. Their common interests, beliefs, and collaboration gave birth to the Catholic Worker Movement. Day attributed the beginnings of the movement to Maurin, but I think that the synergy between these two people enabled things to happen that wouldn't have been possible if either of them had tried to work alone.

Chapter 3, "A Three-Pronged Program of Action," investigates the development of the *Catholic Worker* paper, gives a glimpse of what life would have been like in hospitality houses and farming communes, and emphasizes the importance of retreats that nurtured the development of a lay apostolate and sustained workers within the movement. Day's and Maurin's program of action became an alternative way of living in the modern world and a means to embody

God's love in a society fragmented by divisions of race, ethnicity, gender, and class.

Chapter 4, "A Social Mystic," offers a more careful examination of the social mysticism that informed Day's principled commitments and sustained her activism. Day drew on the insights of mystical writers and fueled her work with prayer and routine spiritual practices. This chapter situates Day's social mysticism within a larger tradition of mysticism in Western Christianity.

Chapters 5 and 6 examine the way in which Day lived by an ethic of peace. Day was so actively engaged in peacemaking activities that her understanding of pacifism cannot be discussed in a single chapter. Chapter 5, "Living by an Ethic of Peace in a Culture Invested in War and Death," discusses Day's expansive definition of pacifism, the theological basis for her peacemaking, and her consistent opposition to war—even during World War II. Chapter 6, "Spreading a Gospel of Peace in the Age of Nuclear War," looks more specifically at her peacemaking activities after World War II, particularly after the United States dropped the atom bomb on Hiroshima and Nagasaki, and then through her work with missions for peace.

Chapter 7, "Looking at Things as a Woman," discusses a controversy among historians and biographers of Day concerning the question of whether or not she should be called a feminist. Historians and biographers of Day more frequently refer to her as a "radical" than a "feminist." However, Dorothy Day believed in the fullness of women's humanity, consistently expressed concern for women living in poverty, lived a nontraditional life for a woman of her era, and recognized that through her activities as an activist and a mother she was a "body well used." Chapter 7 considers Day's feminism by emphasizing her personal and relational understanding of God, considering her early alliance with and later sympathies toward socialism, linking her pacifism with a broader expression of women's activism in the twentieth century, and reflecting on the importance of prophetic mothering. In the context of my discussion, Day's distinctive expression of feminism becomes visible.

This exploration of Dorothy Day's life and the theology and spiritual practices that sustained her activism concludes with my personal comment on "Dorothy Day's Legacy for Contemporary Reformed Christians." The personal postscript may be a distinctive feature of this book when comparing it to others included in the *Armchair Theologians Series*. It is worth explaining why. All of Day's writings included elements of self-disclosure. I could not represent Day's story well if I tried to adopt some sense of objective distance. Her writing, faith commitments, and practices are so engaging that they demand a personal response.

I hope that as you continue reading you will find Dorothy Day as intriguing and fascinating as I did and that you enter into conversation with others about her life experiences, practices, activities, and theology. This book on Day is the first full volume in the Armchair Theologians Series that is devoted to a female theologian. While it is regrettable that female theologians have not been given enough attention in this series, Day's inclusion symbolizes her relevance for our time. In my opinion, Day should not only be remembered as one of the most significant theologians of the twentieth century but as one of the most important theological voices for our time.

Day always insisted that the Catholic Worker was more than a movement for social and economic justice. The Catholic Worker was and continues to be a way of life. Day challenged her societies' disordered priorities and lived with real authenticity and integrity. In our twenty-first century social, economic, and political context, whose story then could be more relevant than Dorothy Day? We are still desperately in need of people of faith who don't just talk the talk, but also walk the walk. What our world needs most are theologians who combine her kind of "street cred" with theological and social imagination.

Author's note: Dorothy Day's writings fit within the genre of spiritual autobiography and are not arranged chronologically. Readers may find it difficult to gain a sense of the chronological development of her ideas. Her life and work in a house of hospitality did not allow her the luxury of time to review, edit, and revise her work with scholarly precision. I have developed a time line that will give readers a better sense of the relationship between noteworthy events in her personal life to events within the Catholic Worker Community, the Roman Catholic Church, as well as in the United States and around the world. The time line can easily be found online at www.catholicworker.org.

CHAPTER ONE

Growing to See the World
in a New Way

Dorothy Day looked at the world through the eyes of the marginalized, the working poor, the single mother, the homeless, the migrant worker, the addict, the prisoner, the pusher, and the prostitute. She was transformed by what these people and their experiences revealed. The concept of *metanoia*—a Greek word meaning a change of mind and used in Christian Scriptures in reference to conversion, turning away from dead works and toward a new relationship with God—figures prominently in her story. Our study of Day's life and practices and the theology that informed and fueled her religious social activism begins with the theme of conversion. Conversion can rarely, if ever, be understood in terms of a single event or as a linear development in a person's journey. Conversion refers to a much longer and gradual process "that stimulates and reflects a powerful and profound change . . . a basic transformation of a person's ways of seeing, feeling, valuing, understanding, and relating."[1]

Day was raised in a family environment that held little commitment to faith or religion. Several members of her family were attracted to socialism and were advocates for workers' rights. Her brother John, like many other socialists, thought religion could be too easily used as a tool to suppress the masses and questioned how anyone could believe that an all-powerful God would permit evil. For many years, Day allied herself with socialist causes and efforts to advocate for workers' rights. In fact, the first jobs she held as a reporter were for socialist newspapers. Dorothy had her brother John in mind when she wrote her first autobiography, *From Union Square to Rome*. The book is a sort of apologia for the Christian faith that Dorothy came to embrace. We may wonder how a woman with little theological training and who was raised in a family that did not nurture religious commitments ultimately grew into one of the most significant and influential lay leaders among twentieth-century American Catholics. How could a journalist who began her career writing for socialist newspapers become one of the most prominent voices in the public forum for *religious* radicals, pacifists, anarchists, and advocates for economic justice? Her conversion story is quite remarkable.

The answer to these questions comes through clearly in *The Long Loneliness*, her second autobiography. By the time Day published this book in 1952, she had matured in her faith and as leader of a movement—the answer to her loneliness and discovery of God came in the form of community. Many people composed the community. Some of them she encountered only briefly, but their faith commitments left a lasting impression on her. Others became mentors and friends who remained with her throughout the weeks, months, and years during which she discerned her vocation in the world. Her relationships with people who she met early on in her life, particularly with those who advocated for workers' rights, revealed to her the "dead works" of social exclusion, class division, racial discrimination, war, and violence. This chapter focuses attention on the early life experiences that contributed to Day's conversion and invites us into the community of people and range of events and places that led her to associate with the masses, to turn away from dead works, and to commit herself to creating a new society.

Childhood "Memories of God"

Reflections on Day's childhood, adolescence, and university days appear under the heading "Searching" in *The Long Loneliness*. Her family relocated four times during her childhood. They lived in Brooklyn, New York; Berkeley and Oakland, California; and Chicago, Illinois. Dorothy and her siblings attended about six different schools. The Days never put down deep roots or developed strong connections to particular places and spaces. Nonetheless, she remembered her childhood as a "happy time" and felt that her immediate family nurtured a sense of continuity with the stories of her ancestors.

Dorothy admitted that as children "we did not search for God."[2] Neither of her parents gave Dorothy or her siblings a model for commitment to a particular faith community. Dorothy recalled: "In the family the name of God was never mentioned. Mother and father never went to church, none of us children had been baptized, and to speak of the soul was to speak immodestly, uncovering what might remain hidden."[3] However, religious thought, institutions, and traditions were not entirely absent from the life of the Day family.

She encountered people who believed in and practiced the Christian faith in different ways—Episcopalians, Congregationalists, Presbyterians, Christian Scientists, and Roman Catholics. It seems reasonable to suggest that the breadth of her exposure to Christianity made her predisposed toward ecumenism. Grace Satterlee Day, Dorothy's mother, was brought up in the Episcopal Church and John Day was raised as a Congregationalist. John's great grandfather, Isaac Day, was involved in the organization of churches and schools in Cleveland, Tennessee. Samuel Houston Day, John's father and the namesake for one of Dorothy's brothers, was a surgeon and served in the Confederate army. He was remembered as a good man who honored, respected, and loved all people equally—"poor and humble" as well as "rich and prosperous." Dorothy held Samuel Houston in high regard because they shared both concern and compassion for those who lacked access to the means to satisfy their own basic needs.[4] Many others felt a sense of admiration for Samuel. Funeral services for her grandfather were held in a Cumberland Presbyterian Church, and the Cleveland paper reported that "'[t]housands of persons' followed the procession to the cemetery."[5]

Both of her parents must have had some interest in questions of faith. It doesn't appear that her parents ever prevented their children from accepting the invitations of others to attend religious services. Grace consulted a Christian Science practitioner when she experienced bouts with headaches while John carried a Bible with him at all times and his sports columns "about racing and racetracks were filled with Biblical and Shakespearean allusions."[6]

There were a few other memorable encounters from her early life with religious people who sparked her curiosity. Day remembered the young Catholic woman who worked for her family in Brooklyn. After they moved to Berkeley, Dorothy went through a phase where she read the Bible to her sister, Della, while they were playing school together in the attic.[7] In Oakland, the Reeds, a Methodist family who lived next door, took Dorothy with them. Dorothy became a "regular churchgoer" for some time.

The Days lived in California until two weeks after the Great San Francisco Earthquake of 1906. It will not surprise you that the earthquake made a lasting impression on Dorothy. She remembered both the cataclysmic damage caused by the earth's vibrations and the way in which people came together in a spirit of solidarity in response to the disaster. Fires ignited across San Francisco and blazed on for several days. Scores of refugees fled the city while it burned. Dorothy described the tremors shaking the ground early in the morning as a "sea which rocked our house in a most tumultuous manner."[8] The earthquake occurred in the early morning. Dorothy was lying in a brass bed when it began vibrating and rolling across the room. Her father quickly grabbed her brothers and ran toward the door. Her mother grabbed Dorothy's sister, Della. Dorothy was left alone in the bed. It took a few moments before Dorothy's parents could get back to her. She didn't remember feeling afraid. What she remembered most about the event was the warmth that she felt as she witnessed people come together in the aftermath of the quake. Her mother and the neighbors "united in Christian solidarity" to provide for the needs of those who lost everything.[9] That experience was formative for Dorothy and contributed later to her own ability to stand in solidarity with others.

The Day family, however, could not stay in that area. John Day had worked as a sports reporter for a newspaper in Oakland. The earthquake destroyed both their home and the plant that printed the newspaper. Two weeks after the earthquake the Days moved to Chicago, where John thought he would have better potential to find work. A good job was not so easily found.

Dorothy said, "It was the first time we had been really poor."[10] Their first home in Chicago was a "dingy, six-room flat" in a tenement district. This early experience of living in a tenement contributed to the sense of compassion

Dorothy felt for people living in poverty. It was there that Dorothy met Mrs. Barrett, a Catholic mother of seven, one of the women who would give Dorothy her "first impulse toward Catholicism." Dorothy liked to play with Catherine Barrett. One day when she went to find Catherine, she entered the Barrett house unannounced after finding no one there to greet her at the door. She found Mrs. Barrett in the front bedroom kneeling in prayer. Dorothy recalled feeling "a burst of love" and "gratitude and happiness" that warmed her heart.[11] Seeing Mrs. Barrett pray piqued Dorothy's curiosity and afterward she tormented her sister Della for many nights with long prayers.

Eventually John Day was hired as a sports editor and worked nights at the *Inter Ocean*. The family could then afford to move to Lincoln Park. They moved into an old house with large rooms. Up until this point, their life "had been one of constant change."[12] This was the first home and space that Dorothy recalled meaning something to her.

While they were living in Lincoln Park, the minister of the Episcopal Church of Our Savior canvassed the neighborhood and found out that Dorothy's mother had been raised in the church. He visited and encouraged the family to attend along with Dorothy. Dorothy doesn't describe every detail related to her attendance at the church, but she was convinced to go long enough to learn the catechism, participate in confirmation class, and to be baptized. She was thirteen years old when she was baptized in the Episcopal Church. "I remember being embarrassed at being baptized," she wrote, "tall gawky girl that I was, and the fact that I was one of many being confirmed did not make me feel any easier."[13]

Her commitment to that congregation lasted about two years. Her mother helped to steer Dorothy's attentions, if only for a brief time, toward Christian Science. Grace became interested in Christian Science when she struggled with depression after Dorothy's brother Donald was born. Dorothy herself was experiencing some headaches and so her mother arranged treatment by a practitioner of Christian Science. Neither Dorothy nor her mother attended the Christian Science Church, but Dorothy did begin reading *Science and Health* as well as other pamphlets published by Christian Science groups. She found the literature of Christian Science just as convincing as "the dogmas of the Episcopalian church."[14]

In her autobiographical writing, Dorothy expressed gratitude that her father allowed her to remain a child, without delegating too much responsibility to her before she was sixteen years old. But it was clear that he didn't want his home to be governed by children. John Day didn't want the children to have friends over to play because additional children would be an intrusion into their private lives. He kept much of the world out of their home. The family didn't have a radio and John encouraged the children of the house to read books by authors that he chose: Victor Hugo, Charles Dickens, Robert Louis Stevenson, and Edgar Allen Poe.[15] Dorothy talked about books as their "only release and outlook"[16] with the exception of the weekly Sunday movie. We can see how Dorothy developed such a strong love for reading and a passion for writing.

Dorothy described her father as a defender of the status quo who distrusted "foreigners" and "agitators" and disagreed with movements that invited rapid social change. His attitude toward "agitators" may explain his later characterization of his daughter in a letter to a friend:

> Dorothy . . . is the nut of the family. When she came out of the university she was a communist. Now she's a Catholic crusader. She owns and runs a Catholic paper and is separated from her husband. . . . I wouldn't have her around me.[17]

Although John's career did not always follow an upward path, Dorothy remembered that her father was proud to have been one of the founders of the Hialeah Park Racetrack in Florida and a published author in the *Saturday Evening Post*.

We can imagine just from this brief description of Dorothy's father that he must not have been an overly affectionate parent. Dorothy was clear in her writing that her father loved his children and she, by her own "intuition," felt his love. Her mother Grace had the task of making and managing the traditional home, sometimes on a shoestring budget. Dorothy shared a close bond with her mother. Grace frequently appears in Dorothy's writings, including her first book, an autobiographical novel titled *The Eleventh Virgin*, as well as in her diaries and other published writings.

When things were really down, Dorothy remembered her mother dressing up for dinner and reigning "over the supper table like a queen." Grace's physical health was an issue for the family. She battled with weakness and frequent headaches. When Dorothy was a teenager, Grace called on her to help with her siblings. Dorothy's youngest brother, John, was born when she was fourteen years old. Dorothy developed a particular affection for him because of the time she helped care for him.

Searching for the Relevance of Classroom Learning

Dorothy graduated at the age of sixteen from Waller High School in Chicago and left home excited to enter the University of Illinois in Urbana. Homesickness soon dulled her excitement and enthusiasm about living away from home, particularly away from her siblings Della and John.

Dorothy's reflections on her days in college focus more on the world around the university than her experience in school. No one can doubt the fact that Dorothy was an avid reader, an intellectually curious person, and a creative thinker. College classes, however, were not as compelling to her as her own struggle to find the world to which she wanted to belong. Moral theologian June O'Connor observes that Dorothy "always seemed to learn more and to learn it more vividly from direct action and direct experience."[18] Day was aware of class differences and economic injustice before she went to college. In high school, she read books that increased her understanding of class consciousness and became acutely aware of the way in which economic and social class affected one's status in society. Day's own experience of independence and freedom during her university days brought the cause of exploited and underpaid workers to life.

Dorothy struggled to make ends meet in college. The *Inter Ocean* failed during Dorothy's first year at the university and so her parents could not afford to pay for her education. Fortunately, Dorothy had taken an examination that was part of a scholarship competition sponsored by the Hearst paper in Chicago during her senior year in high school. Dorothy scored high enough to win a $300 scholarship. It seems unlikely that she would have been able to attend college, even for two years, without this financial assistance. Dorothy had to find different jobs to help pay for additional costs and living expenses. She earned her board by taking up odd jobs, such as helping an impoverished professor and father of five children, washing and ironing clothes, and working in the college cafeteria. During her sophomore year she gained some relief when a friend, Rayna Simons, invited her to live with her as a roommate in a boarding house.

While she was at the university, Dorothy became convinced by Marx's argument that religion was the opiate of the people. She observed, "I wanted to have nothing to do with the religion of those whom I saw all about me. I felt that I must turn from it as from a drug."[19] Neither college nor religion seemed to have anything to do with everyday life. What was more real to her was the struggle of "the masses." Dorothy reveled in being able to choose what she would learn and in defining her own priorities. She described herself as "intoxicated" by her own freedom. She immersed herself in a writing group called the "Scribblers' Club"; designed her own reading list; absorbed the writings of Upton Sinclair, Jack London, Fyodor Dostoyevsky, and Peter Kropotkin; and began to work for Socialist causes.

> I was in love with the masses. I do not remember that I was articulate or reasoned about this love, but it warmed my heart and filled it. It was those among the poor and the oppressed who were going to rise up, they were collectively the new Messiah, and they would release the captives.[20]

Dorothy found a real sense of community with revolutionary friends who were connected by a common cause. She became friends with Rayna Simons and her fiancé at that

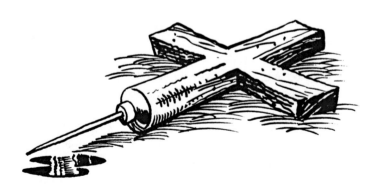

time, Samson Raphaelson or "Raph," who were members of the same writing club as Dorothy. Rayna's father was president of the Chicago Board of Trade and her family was quite wealthy. Despite her wealth, Rayna was not invited to join a sorority, probably because she was Jewish. Dorothy became familiar with the psychological, emotional, and social costs of exclusion through this first brush with anti-Semitism. Throughout her life Dorothy maintained a special sensitivity toward Jewish people and held great respect for the Jewish faith. Later in Dorothy's life when she encountered Christians who thought of their faith as superior to Jews, she would remind them Jesus was a Jew.

Dorothy confessed in *From Union Square to Rome* that she remembered little of what she read or talked about with Rayna and Raph. Her memory of Rayna providing her with shelter and friendship was what she remembered clearly. There were a few other memorable experiences that remained vivid to her. They joined the American Socialist Party. Dorothy attended a few meetings held by the small group of Socialists in the community. They interviewed socialist activist Rose Pastor Stokes for the college paper and met other prominent Socialists such as Scott Nearing, John Masefield, Vachel Lindsay, and Carl Sandburg. After her university days, Rayna made an even stronger commitment to Marxist ideals. She married a radical journalist named William Prohme and together they went to live in China during the years of the Chinese Revolution. Rayna was forced to retreat to Moscow when Chiang Kai-shek took control of the country in 1927. She died in Moscow before her husband could join her there.

In addition to these encounters with socialism and people committed to social reform, Dorothy's oldest brother, Donald, began working at a Socialist newspaper, *The Day Book,* while she was in college. Donald marked the stories in each paper and sent them to his sister to read. The passion of his writing was compelling to her. Dorothy, like so many of her peers, was drawn into the rip currents of social reform.

A Socialist Call

The Day family moved once again in 1916. This time they returned to New York, where her father took a job at the *Morning Telegraph*. Dorothy decided that she would move along with her family and left the University of Illinois in June after completing two years of college-level work. Dorothy lived with her family for a few months until she could find a job as a journalist at the *New York Call*, a Socialist paper.

Finding a job was not easy for her. Her father was not enthusiastic about his daughter (or any woman, for that matter) becoming a journalist. Dorothy wrote, "I had tried other newspapers but without success, in some cases because my father had told his city editor friends to lecture me on the subject of newspaper work for women."[21] John Day must not have accounted for his daughter's persistence. After being turned down at other papers, she succeeded in convincing Chester Wright, an editor at the *New York Call*, to hire her. The editor was reluctant to hire her because of the paper's financial situation. Dorothy's determination led her to propose that she write a series of articles about what it is like to live on five dollars a week. She was inspired by a previous group of New York police who banded together as a "diet squad" to gain some publicity for the city. Newspapers ran stories about their successes as a way of responding to complaints about the high cost of living in New York. Dorothy would be a "diet squad of one" but her mission in this venture was more of an exposé of tenement life. The paper would pay her five dollars a week for a month and, if she was successful, her salary would be raised. Her "Diet Squad" articles focused not only on the challenge of living on five dollars a week but also on the best foods underpaid working people could live on that would give them the strength and "gumption" to fight for better wages. The "Diet Squad" articles ran their course. Dorothy's salary was raised to a whopping ten dollars a week within a few months.

In 1916, New York's East Side was a tenement district and home to many families who had recently immigrated to the United States—Syrians, Italians, Greeks, Germans, Eastern Europeans, and Russians. The city had passed laws two and a half decades before that condemned the tenement buildings, but by some tragedy of inaction or political maneuvering they were still standing. Dorothy described the tenement buildings as filthy and foul smelling with narrow and poorly lit hallways and barely enough room to move about. The smells created by people living together in close quarters hung in the hallway like a drape. She rented a room from the Gottliebs, an Orthodox Jewish family. Her rent was $1.50 a week, paid one month in advance, but there was "no electricity, no bath, no hot water."[22] Somehow the family managed to keep themselves and the apartment clean and smelling of baked goods.

There were other hardships. Tenements were not equipped with central heat. Every family had to heat their own apartment. Fires occurred frequently in the winters. And then there were the bedbugs. In spite of these unhealthy conditions, Dorothy commented, "I enjoyed that winter in the slums and have never lived any place else since. If one must dwell in cities I prefer the slums of the poor to the slums of the rich. A tenement is a tenement whether it is on lower Park Avenue or upper."[23]

Her function as a journalist at the *Call* was to "build up an indictment against the present system."[24] She covered the work of Socialists in legislature, interviewed Socialist leaders, and attended rallies and strikes supported by the Industrial Workers of the World (IWW), the "Wobblies." The IWW touted itself as "a union for all workers" regardless of race, creed, nationality, or gender. Both men and women were among the leadership of the IWW, including William Haywood, Eugene V. Debs, Elizabeth Gurley Flynn, Mary Harris "Mother" Jones, and Lucy Parsons. In Dorothy's judgment, Flynn, a feminist union activist, was the IWW's most effective speaker and advocate. Dorothy attended a number of protests while working as a reporter for the *Call*; one of the last ones before she switched jobs was a peace protest in Washington, DC, planned by Columbia University students. Her next job was working for the Anti-Conscription League, and then later she accepted a position at a Socialist magazine, the *Masses*.

In the fall of 1917, Dorothy went to Washington with the League for the Defense of Political Prisoners to picket the White House. Dorothy recalled two different arrests after two days of protesting. A large group of suffragists had been picketing there for months. The group gathered together before marching on the White House carrying picket signs. Marines grabbed the signs from the hands of the protestors and tore them. They were arrested and then released on bail after the first day of protests. The protestors, Dorothy among them, were arrested on the second day again but refused to post bail. They were held in jail and then sentenced to thirty days at the workhouse in Occoquan.

Occoquan Workhouse was part of a larger experiment aimed toward seeing if hard work was an effective deterrent for short-term prisoners. The workhouse was designed for women who were found guilty of soliciting, prostitution, disorderly conduct, and drunkenness. The fact that Dorothy and the other "pickets" were sent there meant that they were not being treated as political prisoners. When they arrived they were subjected to medical exams, strip searched, given prison clothes, and assigned cells in solitary confinement. There were so many women that two had to share a cell designed for one inmate. Dorothy's cellmate turned out to be Lucy Burns, one of the leaders of the suffrage movement.

All of the women immediately went on a hunger strike, which attracted the attention and garnered the sympathy of the nation. Some of the prisoners were force-fed during the strike. Fortunately for Dorothy, the prison guards saved this cruelty for the suffrage leaders and organizers of the protest. After a few days in prison, Dorothy asked one of the guards for a Bible to read and she read the Psalms. She described the feeling of being "abandoned by God" as she read the Bible within the context of the workhouse. She felt ashamed that she turned to God in the midst of her despair. Thoughts of teachers, friends, colleagues, and members of her own family who were convinced of the corruption of religion were undoubtedly also in her mind. The strike lasted for ten days and ended only because local officials met the demands made by the women to be treated as political prisoners. They were given street clothes, books, and moved to a Washington jail. After sixteen days, President Woodrow Wilson pardoned all of them.

Did Dorothy find a sense of community among the women suffragists? There is some discussion among historians and theologians about whether or not Day can or should be called a feminist. A fuller discussion of the way in which Day's commitments and feminist convictions converge will have to wait for another chapter. But it is worth mentioning at this point that she did not feel a strong connection to the suffrage movement. Her first allegiance was to workers, and she voiced sympathies for mistreated prisoners. While in jail, she felt "the cause for which we were in jail seemed utterly unimportant. I had not much interest in the vote, and it seemed to me our protest should have been not for ourselves but for all those thousands of prisoners throughout the country, victims of a materialistic system."[25] The imprisonment of the women suffragists at the Occoquan Workhouse is remembered today as a turning point in the suffrage movement. News of the brutal treatment of the suffragists at Occoquan provoked widespread public outcry in support of civil disobedience. Even though Dorothy

stood among the protestors and witnessed the passage of the nineteenth amendment, she herself never exercised the right to vote.[26]

Dorothy returned to New York after her release from prison and worked as a freelance writer for some time. Later she began to work for the *Liberator,* the magazine that was the successor to the *Masses.* Through her work as a reporter for Socialist publications, Dorothy found herself part of a community of radical reporters and writers in Greenwich Village. Editors Mike Gold and Max Eastman, publishers Charles and Albert Boni, and famous playwright Eugene O'Neill were her comrades and companions for long evenings debating around tables at restaurants or in local bars.

In the winter of 1917, the editors of the *Masses* were taken to trial by the state and Dorothy was called as a witness. A succession of events, including the trial, led her to seek community elsewhere. She, along with her sister, Della, applied for admission to nursing school at King's County Hospital in Brooklyn.

A Disappointing Love Affair

1918 was the year of the Spanish flu epidemic. Records of the U.S. National Archives show that the flu epidemic killed an estimated 50 million people that year. No place in the United States was granted immunity as the flu spread in urban and rural communities from the East Coast to Alaska. After 1918, the average life expectancy of citizens dropped by twelve years; twenty-five percent of the population was afflicted.

Dorothy served as a nurse trainee in the county hospital during that year. Serving as a nurse in the county hospital was difficult work. Every day eight to ten patients "were carried in or walked in staggeringly" to the ward where

Dorothy worked. Dorothy and other trainees worked twelve-hour days. When they had breaks they were often required to listen to lectures about human anatomy or on topics related to other aspects of their training.

One of the other nurse trainees was a young Catholic woman named Miss Adams. In *The Long Loneliness*, Dorothy wrote about the way Miss Adams reminded her of Mrs. Barrett. Dorothy began to associate "her natural goodness and ability with her Catholicism."[27] Their training at the hospital was intended to create order and discipline, and Dorothy appreciated the daily rhythm of the work. Making beds, bathing patients, rubbing them with alcohol, dressing bed sores, distributing medicines, and assisting with other treatments were all done on a precise schedule.

The record that Dorothy offers of her work as a nurse at King's County is limited in two of her autobiographical works, *From Union Square to Rome* and *The Long Loneliness*. She makes no mention of her sister, Della, who also signed up for the course at the hospital, or of her affair with a kitchen orderly named Lionel Moise. This period of her life was a time in which she felt a strong desire and attraction to goodness, but she fumbled and made mistakes that she later regretted. A more detailed, yet disguised, account of the story of her romance with Moise is told in *The Eleventh Virgin*, her autobiographical novel, which allowed Dorothy to take some emotional distance from her experience by masking herself as the character "June Henreddy."

Lionel Moise, a.k.a. Dick Wemys in *The Eleventh Virgin*, created a tumult within Dorothy that led to a love of wild abandon. Moise had worked for a moving company in Caracas before serving as an orderly in the hospital. Dorothy described him as an adventurous soul. She was immediately attracted to his crooked nose, "sort of hacked off so that it looked as though it were pushed to one side." They shared the adventure of working on a ward together calming and sometimes controlling delirious and unruly patients.

It is difficult to say how much Dorothy embellished the story about her love affair with Lionel in *The Eleventh Virgin*. Some of the script seems out of character for a woman who later became well known for her leadership as a *religious* social activist.

> "I am becoming a common little slut," June maintained. "I slink out at night without telling anyone where I am going and meet you on deserted streets, and we have so little time together that I catch myself scheming."[28]

We might find it surprising that Dorothy so thinly veiled her attraction to Lionel in the character of June. Most people fear telling others about their own scheming and the way they calculate decisions to win someone else's affection.

Dorothy admitted that throughout their relationship Lionel pushed her away as much as he pulled her close. When he left his job as an orderly at the hospital he invited Dorothy to live with him as "his woman," a title that she found "delightfully humiliating." She intended to go immediately to his apartment but was delayed when her mother became ill. Once she was able to make her way to his apartment, she found him welcoming even though he was a bit perturbed by her delay.

While they lived together they enjoyed passion and companionship but not true partnership. He expected her to wait on him "hand and foot." Their relationship lacked either the covenant or commitment to endure. Lionel did not seem to understand commitment or maybe he was incapable of it. His character, Dick, said things like, "I love you . . . I can't say how I will feel tomorrow." "I do love you . . . but I can get along without you." These patronizing remarks didn't seem to throw up enough red flags to make Dorothy flee in escape. There were bouts with jealousy, arguments, and at least one temporary breakup in their relationship. Dorothy didn't confront the real impermanence of their relationship until she became pregnant. You can probably predict the ending of this story.

Lionel would not consent to having a child. Dorothy had conflicted feelings. She suppressed her feelings about having the baby and had an abortion. Her abortion is a flashpoint for discussion among contemporary commentators, particularly for Catholics, because of the Roman Catholic Church's stance on abortion. Dorothy later came to regret her decision to have an abortion but realized that the experience also contributed to her own transformation. She came to understand the importance of community just as much in the midst of people who loved her and nurtured her as in the days of alienation and depth of despair she knew at the end of her affair with Lionel.

After her relationship with Lionel ended, Dorothy went back to work in the hospital for a while. She felt a longing to return to writing, however, and later held jobs in New York, Chicago, and New Orleans. The disappointment that she felt in her relationship with Lionel led her to seek the affirmation of another man. She married Berkeley Tobey and they traveled together for about a year in Europe. They divorced after they returned to the United States.

After leaving Tobey, Day was drawn to Chicago, where her old flame Lionel Moise had a job as an editor for the *Chicago Post*. Day took whatever work she could find to support herself for a while and then finally landed as a secretary for one of the editors at the *Liberator*. The paper and other socialist organizations in the city were under close federal surveillance. On occasion Day would stay at a house owned by the IWW. She was jailed for a second time in July

1922 after a raid by the police "Red Squad" on the house where she was staying with her friend Marie Cramer.[29]

Many people who were suspected of being "radicals" were arrested, jailed, and some even deported. Dorothy and Marie, along with other women, were transported in a paddy wagon to the jail and treated as prostitutes. Neither Marie nor Dorothy had a lawyer or anyone who could pay their bail, so after their first court appearance they were sent to the city jail. After her arraignment in court, she was sent to another jail where a drug addict in the cell next to her was going through a forced detoxification of her system and spent the night wailing in agony. Dorothy wrote, "No woman in childbirth, no cancer patient, no one in the long year I had spent in King's County Hospital had revealed suffering like this. . . . To see human beings racked, by their own will, made one feel the depth of the disorder of the world."[30] That experience remained with Day and shaped her understanding of what people in prison face during their incarceration.

After her release from prison, Moise helped Day get a job at the city news bureau of the *Chicago Post* where she "wrote feature stories, covered night courts, divorce courts, interviewed the wives of criminals and the mothers of men about to be hung."[31] During the time she lived there, she roomed with three other women who were practicing Catholics. She was intrigued by and drawn to the devotional practices of her roommates but, at that time, stopped short of committing to a religious community.

Day returned to New York for a brief time when Moise moved away from Chicago. In December 1923, she moved to New Orleans with her sister, Della, and a friend of theirs named Mary. Day found employment there at another newspaper. Her book *The Eleventh Virgin* was published in 1924. Although she had promises from prominent writers like Eugene O'Neill to endorse the book, it received poor reviews and she even referred to it as "a bad novel." The book was important for her in that in many ways she made peace with the tumult of her youth and it contributed to her conversion.[32] She returned to New York in 1924 after she sold the story from *The Eleventh Virgin* for $5,000 for moving-picture rights. Although the movie was never made, the money she made from the sale of the story enabled her to buy a small cottage on Staten Island.

New Birth

Back in New York, Day easily found a circle of support and community among old friends, particularly Peggy and Malcolm Cowley and Kenneth and Lily Burke. Lily introduced Dorothy to Forster Batterham, the man who later became Dorothy's common-law husband. Forster was from Asheville, North Carolina and had attended the University of Georgia. During World War I he served in the army, but spent most of the war hospitalized due to influenza. Dorothy felt that "it was life with him that brought me natural happiness, that brought me to God."[33]

She makes an intriguing claim about Forster bringing her to God. Forster was a biologist and an anarchist. His interests in biology opened Dorothy's eyes to the beauty and complexity of the natural world. They both shared a reverence for nature, but Forster balked when she marveled at or mused of God's handiwork in the midst of creation. Forster argued for and defended total freedom in body and in soul. He was an anarchist who rebelled against human-made institutions, especially marriage, traditional norms of family, and the church.

Forster and Dorothy sustained and bolstered their relationship through individual freedom and partnership. Their partnership, rather "comradeship," to use Dorothy's words, must have been refreshing after the disappointing end to her life with Moise. She and Forster lived together at their beach house. He usually left during the week to go into the city to work. Dorothy stayed and read her morning paper, took walks along the beach, and listened to the sound of the sea crashing against the shore. On weekends they hosted Communist friends for beach parties and bohemian-style gatherings where a critical appreciation of literature often became the focus of conversation.

The depth and breadth of her relationship with Forster made Dorothy happy. She began to pray out of her happiness rather than out of the depths of despair she had experienced before. Forster's role in bringing her closer to God became even more evident when Dorothy became pregnant. "God is Creator and the very fact that we were begetting a child made me have a sense that we were made in the image and likeness of God, co-creators . . ."[34] As you can imagine, a rebellious spirit like Forster did not instantly warm to the idea of having a baby. Apparently, though, he accustomed himself to the idea over time.

Their daughter, Tamar Teresa, was born in March 1926. Dorothy chose the name Tamar, which means "little palm tree" in Hebrew, because it was included in the genealogy of Jesus in Matthew's Gospel. Their daughter's middle name, Teresa, was connected with two saints, Teresa of Avila and Thérèse of Lisieux. Teresa of Avila was a Spanish mystic, author of *The Interior Castle,* and known for her practice of mental prayer. A woman occupying the bed next to Dorothy while she was in the hospital also gave her a medal of the Little Flower to pin on the baby. The woman, a Catholic, identified the name Teresa with Thérèse of Lisieux.

After Tamar's birth, Dorothy could not suppress her desire to have her daughter baptized. Sister Aloysia, a Sister of Charity, arranged for Tamar to be baptized in a church in Tottenville, New York, in July 1927. Aloysia told Dorothy that she too "must be baptized" even though Dorothy had already been baptized at the age of thirteen in the Episcopal Church. The canons governing the Catholic Church define baptism as *de fide definita* ("of defined faith"), meaning that it is to be administered once and only once. There are, however, two reasons why someone could be re-baptized or, to use the terminology defined in the canons, "conditionally baptized." First, conditional baptism would be warranted if the baptism was not done using the traditional Trinitarian formula in the name of Father, Son, and Holy Spirit. Second, if the one being baptized did so with what might be considered improper intentions and the doctrine of baptism had not been explained properly, that person could be conditionally baptized. The Episcopal Church uses the traditional Trinitarian formula for baptism. It seems most likely then that Dorothy was conditionally baptized because of her own intentions or that the doctrine of baptism had not been properly explained to her.

The story of the execution of two men, Ferdinando Nicola Sacco and Bartolomeo Vanzetti, is placed somewhat awkwardly in Dorothy's record of the events leading up to her own baptism. Sacco and Vanzetti were Italian-born immigrants, labor leaders, activists, and Roman Catholics. They had been active in many struggles for worker's rights, taken part in demonstrations, and organized strikes or protests of their own. Along with other comrades, Sacco and Vanzetti began to organize a public protest in Boston after the suicide of a friend and fellow labor activist, Andrea Salsedo. While they were trying to garner support for the protest among other radicals, the two men were arrested and accused of stealing nearly $16,000 from Slater and Morrill Shoe Company and killing two security guards on duty at the shoe factory during the robbery. Sacco and Vanzetti were convicted of the crimes and sentenced to death by electrocution. Many believed that they were framed. Felix Frankfurter, a future Supreme Court Justice, and Upton Sinclair, among other well-known United States citizens, spoke out publicly in their defense. Protests were staged all over the world—Boston, New York, London, Amsterdam. Workers demonstrated by walking out on their jobs in Tokyo. There were riots in South America, Paris, Geneva, and Johannesburg. On the day they were executed Dorothy described the nation's grief:

> All the nation mourned . . . I mean that is made up of the poor, the worker, the trade unionist—those who felt most keenly the sense of solidarity—that very sense of solidarity which made me gradually understand the doctrine of the Mystical Body of Christ whereby we are the members one of another.[35]

And yet the Catholic Church had not come to their defense. Dorothy felt a special empathy for these men as labor leaders and Catholics.

She accused the church of being "lined up with property, with the wealthy, with the state, with capitalism, with all the forces of reaction," but she believed that the church also made Christ visible in the world. She wanted "to die in order to live, to put off the old man and put on Christ." In August, she left Tamar in her sister's care and went to the church in Tottenville to be baptized. Dorothy was conditionally baptized in the Catholic Church on December 29, 1927, just a few months after Tamar.

Forster was vexed by her decision. She was aware that Forster could not support her decision but not fully conscious of how his resistance would affect her emotionally. Forster left her and Tamar. Dorothy wrote letters to Forster pleading with him to change his mind, consent to marry her, and be a father to Tamar. But, the "irrevocable acts" of their baptism meant that Dorothy had chosen a life in which she and Tamar would be left to make their way together without the daily presence of Forster.

Around this time, the Pathé movie studio located in California offered Dorothy a job as a writer. The offer to work for the movie studio gave Day some time to escape from the tension she felt with Forster because of his unwillingness to change his perspective and marry her. While in California, they kept in touch through letters and Day made it clear that she was trying to "bulldoze" Forster into marrying her.[36] The movie studio proved disappointing. There wasn't enough work for her to do. Dorothy and Tamar drifted for a while after leaving California and before landing again in New York. Dorothy took Tamar with her to

Mexico. They lived there for about six months, but were forced to return to the United States after learning that Tamar had contracted malaria. They lived for a brief time in New Jersey with some friends and then, in the fall of 1931, moved to Coral Gables, Florida to live with Dorothy's mother. Her father was on assignment in Cuba during that time. Day returned to New York in 1932 and eventually took up residence in an apartment with her younger brother, John, and his new wife, Tessa.

New Beginning

Dorothy's early experience working in radical social movements led her to associate herself with "the masses, in loving and praising God." She did not join the Roman Catholic Church because she was attracted to its intellectual traditions or aesthetic sophistication. The Catholic Church attracted her because it "was the Church of the poor, . . . had been built from the pennies of servant girls, that cared for the emigrant, it established hospitals, orphanages, day nurseries, houses of the Good Shepherd, homes for the aged."[37]

Historians and theologians often point to Day's baptism as the event that marked her earnest pursuit of her vocation as a religious social activist. Her baptism represents a distinct turning point in her conversion, but her conversion is best understood as a lifelong process. Dorothy had already contemplated for some time her own receptivity to God. Her baptism was as much a culmination of events from her early life as it was a new beginning. Through her baptism she witnessed publicly to her own change of mind; she also signaled to others her belief that the world in which she lived was prone to "dead works." June O'Connor, a Catholic moral theologian, points out, "God was no longer an element in her consciousness, God was now the ground and all else the figure."[38] The love and sensitivity, natural happiness, she experienced with Forster and after Tamar's birth gave her the first taste of a community that could satisfy the hungry heart. The means to create a community that would satisfy the needs of other hungry people around her was still to come in her consciousness. She would not discover a "plan of action" until she met a French peasant named Peter Maurin who became her friend and mentor. Together, Maurin and Day set out to unleash the "church's social dynamite"; a power inspired by the life, death, and resurrection of Christ.

CHAPTER TWO

Synergy

While Day began to look at the world through the lenses of the marginalized early in her life, developing a mature understanding of the relevance of Christian faith to her social concern was a lifelong process. Peter Maurin, a French peasant and philosopher, helped Day to synthesize her social concern with Catholic faith. She met Peter in 1932, the year that the stock market bottomed out during the Great Depression. Maurin came to Day with a "program of action" in mind that included the creation of a paper, roundtable discussion groups to disseminate their ideas, and houses of hospitality and farming communes to welcome and support people in need. He "disturbed her content," to use Day's own words. The previous chapter identified a continuous flow of people who moved in and out of Day's life and shaped her thought and actions. This chapter will focus on one key figure, Peter Maurin.

Day herself attributed the beginning of the Catholic Worker Movement to Maurin. However, she had a more visionary role. She still maintains a place as the icon and charismatic leader of the movement in the broader academy and within church communities. She wrote about the influence of Maurin's philosophical abstractions and at the same time observed that to her, "being a woman, the ideas were not dynamic unless they were illustrated with incident."[1] In this chapter we will investigate the life and thought of Maurin and his influence on Day's way of thinking and formation.

The life and thought of both Maurin and Day reveal a theologically rich worldview. Their common belief that Christian faith and practice provided an alternative way of dealing with modern social problems enabled them to forge a partnership through which a movement could be born.

A Timely Introduction

Peter and Dorothy met for the first time in December 1932 in Day's apartment in New York where she lived with her brother John, his wife, Tessa, and her daughter, Tamar. She had just returned home from a trip to Washington to report on two significant events, the Hunger March of the Unemployed and a farmers' convention that brought together small farmers and tenant farmers from all around the United States. The *Commonweal* and *America*, both progressive Catholic magazines, had commissioned articles on these events. Day recalled in *The Long Loneliness* that the demonstrations were "Communist inspired" and there was a swell of resistance to them among city officials. When the marchers were finally allowed to take to the streets, Day watched with great pride. The marchers demanded "Work, not Wages," unemployment insurance, plans for people who were disabled and elderly, and relief for women and children. Day went to the National Shrine at the Catholic University to pray after witnessing the march. She prayed both for the marchers but also "that some way would open up for me to use what talents I possessed for my fellow workers, for the poor."[2]

Maurin sought out Day because he had read some of the articles she wrote for publications like the *Sign* and *Commonweal*. She described him as a "short, stocky man in his mid-fifties, as ragged and rugged as any of the marchers."[3] Their meeting could not have been more timely. Day had committed herself to Catholicism five years earlier. She had explored the traditions and rituals of the church and encountered the mystical writers but had not yet fully discovered or integrated the social message of her faith with her own practice. Maurin was also looking for a partner to enact his ideas. He helped Day to see ancient Christian traditions and practices as the means to resist the depersonalizing, dehumanizing, and divisive aspects of modern society. Day brought her practical experience to the partnership.

Economic Disparities in the 1930s

Many people think of 1929, the year the stock market crashed, as the nadir of the Great Depression. However, the market dropped to its lowest point in 1932, the year that Maurin and Day met. By 1933, one fourth of United States residents who wanted to work were unable to find employment. Those who could find a job were often forced to work for the lowest possible pay without any benefits. No federal minimum wage existed at that time. The Fair Labor Standards Act was not passed by Congress until 1938, despite many earlier efforts to regulate work hours and wages. Entitlements and safety nets such as social security, food stamps, and unemployment insurance were not available. There were few programs that were designed to address, even temporarily, the needs of families living in poverty. People all over the United States were living in desperate poverty. Lack of access to family-sustaining employment meant that waves of people were forced to migrate across the country as they searched for work. Farmers from the Midwest became symbols of those who were forced to migrate. In the 1930s, weather destroyed crops all across the Great Plains, forcing the farmers and their families to move. By 1940, about 2.5 million people had been forced to move out of the plains states in what came to be known as the Dust Bowl exodus.[4] Many transferred from the Midwest and Southwest to California. Photojournalists like Dorothea Lange captured the feelings of people living in poverty in photographs of families living in ramshackle houses built from scrap wood and snapshots of hungry children clothed in rags and standing on bare feet. The Great Depression left an indelible psychological imprint on the generation of United States residents who grew up during those lean years.

Wealth was funneled toward those at the top of the economic ladder at the same time that poverty swelled among those being pushed to the bottom. Economist Hugh Rockoff observes that the great fortunes that were made in the Gilded Age were the result of several factors, including "the diffusion of new manufacturing technology" and the "potential for the investors and entrepreneurs . . . to make or increase their fortunes through investments in booming real estate and financial markets."[5] Remember the legendary wealth of John Jacob Astor, Andrew Carnegie, and John D. Rockefeller? At the time of his death in 1937, John D. Rockefeller's fortune of $192 billion dollars[6] equaled about 1.53 percent of the total United States annual gross domestic product. Capitalists who amassed such wealth were known to their critics at the time as "robber barons." Keep in mind that in 1937, the nation was recovering from the Great Depression, unemployment still hovered around 14.3 percent, and, according to the Bureau of Labor Statistics, the average laborer earned about fifty-two cents per hour. It was not until 1941, when the United States entered into World War II, that unemployment dropped below 10 percent.

George Schuster, editor of *Commonweal*, was one of the people who had encouraged Maurin to introduce himself to Day because he thought they would "think alike." Maurin and Day shared concerns about poverty, the impact of industrialism on workers, widespread wealth inequalities, and the role that religious people should play in addressing these problems. According to Maurin, one of the main problems with the modern world was that people and the societies in which they lived had forsaken the common good in favor of individual progress. Fortunes made by the robber barons (despite the good philanthropic deeds of industrialists like Rockefeller and Carnegie) certainly support his point. The rugged individualism that characterized the early twentieth century had led to the fragmentation of community. Maurin drew on personalist philosophy and the concepts of the works of mercy and voluntary poverty as he envisioned a program that would create a society where it was easier for people to be good.

Maurin's ideas were based on a medieval synthesis that advocated for the use of reason to arrive at an end of eternity in the midst of time. He argued that Christians should follow Jesus' teachings about caring for the marginalized in society. The Roman Catholic Church ensconced Jesus' teaching found in Matthew 25:31–46 in the doctrine of the works of mercy. Traditionally, the works of mercy have been divided into two categories, the corporal works of mercy and spiritual works of mercy. Corporal works of mercy include feeding the hungry, giving drink to the thirsty, sheltering the homeless, clothing the naked, visiting prisoners, caring for the sick, and burying the dead. Stories about the apostles and saints illustrated the many ways Christians had chosen to care for the poor, even by voluntarily becoming poor. If Christians were to continue the apostles' acts of healing, weren't works of mercy and voluntary poverty relevant to modern social and economic problems? Peter Maurin unequivocally responded "yes."

Industrialization, technological advance, dependence on wage labor, among other things, had created divisions among people and between people and the land. Modern society needed to return to a lands-and-crafts model where people saw themselves as members of a community and sustained themselves by the land. Maurin had been formed by his experience of growing up in a rural predominantly Catholic community in France just as Christian socialism was making significant progress in that country. His ideas were shaped by his faith and education in Catholic schools as well as by popular intellectual currents and his involvement in people's movements of his time. Maurin schooled himself in personalist philosophy and ancient and medieval history, eagerly consumed books on Christian theology, and experienced living as part of a communitarian group. Maurin believed that workers had to turn themselves into scholars and scholars had to become workers for real change to occur.

A Worker-Scholar

Born in 1877, Maurin was one of twenty-four children born to his parents. They lived in the small town of Oultet, France. As a teenager he received some education and training from the Christian Brothers, a male religious order founded and organized by Jean-Baptiste de La Salle. Maurin went to the Christian Brothers' school near Paris and then after five years began teaching there. Nearly all of the parish schools supported by the order were involved in teaching poor children.

While he was growing up, Peter would have also encountered a large Christian movement that was emerging in France to advocate for Christian alternatives to the economics of industrial capitalism. In 1891, Pope Leo XIII, who later became known as the "working-man's pope," published an encyclical entitled *Rerum Novarum*, "Of New Things," that stated the Catholic Church's position on promoting human dignity through the just distribution of wealth. Among other things, the encyclical identified the condition of laborers as the most pressing question for the churches. Society should be organized and governed so as to enable each individual to better his or her own condition "to the utmost in body, soul, and property." *Rerum Novarum* emphasized the mission of Catholic associations to help "people in poverty out of their difficulties." Organizations were founded all over France to confront economic injustices and address the plight of workers, including the Roman Catholic Society of Social Economy, the Union of Social Peace, and Working Men's Clubs.

Maurin worked for years as a manual laborer and had firsthand experience of life as an immigrant when he left France for Canada, and then, after a few years of living in Canada, immigrated to the United States. In 1909, Maurin went to Canada at least in part out of the desire to have an opportunity to make a living off the land and to build an alternative type of community. He worked in a number of jobs, first as a thresher and then later with the Canadian Pacific Railroad. He settled for some time with the Doukhobors ("Spirit Wrestlers"), a communitarian group who called themselves the Christian Community of Universal Brotherhood. The Doukhobors settled in Canada when the country offered them asylum after they experienced religious and political persecution in their native country of Russia. Their beliefs and practices were based on a literal reading of the Gospels. The Doukhobors made their living by farming and became known for advocating internationalism, pacifism, communism, and vegetarianism. Maurin wrote little about these early experiences. However, some of his later arguments about returning to a lands-and-crafts society and living on farming communes bear the imprint of his brief interlude among the Doukhobors.

In 1911, Maurin headed from Canada to the United States by hopping aboard trains or stowing away in empty freight cars. As an immigrant in the United States, it was difficult for him at the time to find steady employment. He worked in a variety of cities, at first in primarily low-wage jobs such as janitor or dry goods clerk, before he found more steady and well-paying employment as a French tutor in Chicago. Low-wage work ensured a kind of chronic instability in his life and living in poverty in the United States made a lasting impression on him. Poverty itself wasn't a new experience for Maurin. What differed about his experience of poverty in the United States was that "being poor in this country of material promise and progress was in fact a crime."[7] During the years he was migrating, he was arrested on more than one occasion: for vagrancy, when neighbors of people from whom he asked for help suspected that he was a thief, and by railroad detectives, among other things.[8]

Influenced by Popular Intellectual Currents

About five years before Maurin introduced himself to Day, he took a job working as a handyman at a Catholic boys camp in upstate New York. Maurin was unable to invest much energy in the church during the years that he spent so much time in transit. His job at the camp renewed his commitment to the Catholic Church. Around 1927 Maurin also began writing "Easy Essays," which were digests of his thought written in poetic form.

Day worked on a biography of Maurin for many years but never completed the project in her lifetime. After she died, Francis J. Sicius published Day's manuscript along with his own commentary on Maurin as *Peter Maurin: Apostle to the World*. Sicius includes some of the "little essays" to which Day referred in her biography of Maurin as well as some additional essays that she did not reference. The essays offer good, short summaries of Maurin's thought and vision for a new world order and show evidence of his intellectual curiosity and attraction to philosophy.

Maurin was an avid reader and was influenced by the work of French philosopher Jacques Maritain, the Russian exile Nikolai Berdyaev, and, particularly, by the personalist Emmanuel Mounier. Both Maritain and Mounier made distinctive contributions to French social and political thought in the 1930s. Maritain fought to integrate politics with morality and the Christian message. Mounier is widely recognized as one of the guiding spirits behind personalist philosophy. Personalism was an expression of disdain for the political and economic structures as they were evolving in the early twentieth century. Maurin, in his essay "Personalist Communitarianism," described the personalist as "other-centered" and "spreading the doctrine of the common good through words and deeds." Personalism, as a philosophy, sought to bring human personality into greater harmony with the material world. It was in this way a direct response to philosophies of materialism that were popular at the time—fascism, communism, and bourgeois capitalism.

An Alternative Vision

Maurin thought that a socially and economically responsible Christianity was best lived out by individuals making countless personal choices for the common good. He used colorful metaphors and vivid language to emphasize the urgent need for change. He said it was time to "blow the dynamite of the Church's social message" in the midst of the modern world and to turn "parish domes into parish homes." Preparing people to take responsibility for other people to whom they were intrinsically related bore the greatest potential to heal fragmented communities. He wrote, "There was a time in the history of the church . . . when it organized social welfare for the community. For the poor there were daily meals; for the homeless there were houses of hospitality."[9] In the past, the needs of individuals were considered in relation to a larger whole.

The timing of Maurin's and Day's meeting was of great significance. Day felt that Christians were too passive in the face of the workers' oppression. Maurin believed that there was a way that Christianity could be made credible again in modern society. He had already adopted a lifestyle similar to Francis of Assisi. Francis was the son of a rich textile merchant and was remembered by the church for rejecting his father's wealth, living a contemplative life, voluntarily adopting a life of poverty, and celebrating the sacredness of the whole creation. Like Francis, Maurin lived without the encumbrance of material possessions and discovered that he had more freedom to study, pray, and meditate.

Day admitted that at first the two had difficulty understanding each other. Peter was fifty-five years old when they met and Dorothy was only about thirty-six. He resisted Communist materialism and opposed the collective bargaining of unions. Day had been part of the socialist movement and defended the right of workers to organize. Maurin had worked primarily as a manual laborer, although he also sometimes made a living as a teacher or tutor. Day had made her living primarily as a writer. Historian Anne Klejment identifies other differences in their perspectives that became more evident as their ideas formed into a full-fledged movement. Maurin was a strict personalist who thoroughly distrusted government. Day was more likely to accept government reforms and assistance programs that could benefit people living in poverty. She enthusiastically endorsed the work of labor unions; Catholic Workers supported strikers in a number of ways, including standing on the picket line and helping to feed and fund picketers. In the mid-1930s the Catholic Workers founded a labor school in New York. Peter was more skeptical about unions. "Strikes don't strike me," he said. He feared that the real goal of the unions was to expand the bourgeoisie.[10]

Despite the difficulties they faced at first in communicating with one another, they soon discovered common passions. They shared the belief that the gospel stories introduced an alternative vision for reality from the consumerism and competition imposed on society by market capitalism.

Maurin came to Day's apartment with a specific program of action in mind that would inspire a lay apostolate to live out the church's social teachings. At the beginning of the chapter, I mentioned that Day considered Maurin the visionary and founder of the Catholic Worker Movement. However, Day did not come to this partnership empty-handed. Day and Maurin were co-collaborators who worked together to form a movement and implement a three-pronged

program of action—raising consciousness and fostering a new vision through a newspaper and weekly roundtable discussions, hospitality houses, and family communes. Day contributed her own skills as a writer, editor, and activist along with her interests in urban life and building relationships among people living in poverty. Maurin never personally served on the bread line. His real passion was for returning to an economic system that was not based on profit but on sustaining individuals and communities through the land. Their synergistic relationship enabled things to be accomplished that may not otherwise have been achievable.

CHAPTER THREE

A Three-Pronged Program of Action

Since Day's first real employment was as a journalist for radical socialist newspapers, it is not surprising that when Maurin came to Day with a program of action in mind, the newspaper was the first part of the plan to be implemented. Historians and biographers may debate whether or not Maurin should be named as the founder of the Catholic Worker Movement, but they agree that the paper was unequivocally Day's. When Maurin met Day they talked about a larger, three-pronged program of action. The newspaper would play a key role in disseminating creative ideas, raising consciousness about the relevance of Christianity to social problems, and building support among the masses for a movement.

Neither of them ever laid out a clear strategic plan or created a budget to initiate and fund other aspects of the program; it emerged in an organic way. The movement began with a consciousness of poverty and a paper to share ideas. During roundtable discussions and in their writing they thought about how the Gospel narratives identified the means for peace and then reflected on these teachings in light of the tremendous need they saw in the city around them. They opened their home to provide shelter for people who were homeless. The soup line first began because one of the workers who had been tending the clothes closet ran out of clothing to distribute, so he began inviting people to sit down and have a cup of coffee. In a television interview on *Christopher Closeup*, Day observed, "If your [own] brother is hungry you feed him." You don't send him away to "wait for a week until he gets a welfare check. You feed him." From Dorothy's perspective, Jesus had left himself to his followers in the form of food, bread, and wine. Who then could be turned away and left hungry? The beginning of the soup line was both as simple and as difficult as that.

This chapter focuses on the development of the *Catholic Worker* newspaper, the importance of both writing and artwork for reaching readers, and life in hospitality houses and farming communes, and it begins to outline the spiritual practices that sustained those participating in the Catholic Worker Movement. Each of these activities raised consciousness about the systemic and structural causes of poverty in the United States and responded to the immediate needs of people within the local community. The main intent, however, was not to establish a social service organization or to form an advocacy group. Day and Maurin wanted to build up a new order that would eventually replace free market capitalism, fueled as it was by greed, with the reign of love. Their program of action became the means to embody God's love and to live as a new society without boundaries imposed by divisions of race, ethnicity, and class.

Writing as an Act of Love

Catholic Worker Jim Forest, a friend of Day's and the paper's editor for a time, observed that "more than anything else, Dorothy was a writer . . . Note-taking and journal keeping was as much a part of Dorothy as breathing."[1] Writing can be distracting and can occupy a tremendous amount of time. Those who discover writing to be their vocation, a calling from God, often find their thoughts consumed by ideas for or about issues needing to be addressed in their next article or book. This was certainly true for Day. Writing was one of the primary ways that Day addressed "the masses." She confessed in the beginning of *Thérèse*, her book on the saint from Lisieux, that she did not take the time that a scholar would to go back and meticulously check details. Her articles and books were written with popular audiences in mind and, more importantly, with the hope of contributing to the formation of a lay apostolate.

Maurin originally suggested that the paper be called the *Catholic Radical* or the *Catholic Agronomist*. As editor of the paper, Day thought the *Catholic Worker* was a better name and chose it because the name "worker" was common to both Catholics and socialists. There was also a socialist paper being circulated at that time that was called the *Daily Worker.* Her title signaled their solidarity, as Christians, with workers who were struggling for fair wages or to find adequate employment. Paulist Press, a Catholic publisher, set the type and printed 2,500 copies of the first edition of the paper for $57.00. The first issue made strong and clear connections between Christian faith and the plight of the workers by taking up issues related to economic justice, the social teachings of the church, and nonviolence.

Maurin, however, was disappointed in the first issue of the *Catholic Worker.* He wanted a stronger emphasis on the philosophy that undergirded their work. The paper was intended to unlock the "social dynamic force" of the church's message. Day was more practically oriented and preferred to avoid focusing only on philosophical abstractions. Maurin's first response: "A paper for everybody is a paper for nobody." Their disagreements led Maurin to step away for a brief time. He tried to begin his own hospitality house in Harlem but eventually returned to work with Day.

Day put together the first edition of the *Catholic Worker* at her kitchen table after supper, at the library, and in the park while she watched her daughter, Tamar, play. At times, she found writing to be a harrowing experience because it took time away from the work of serving those around her in more concrete ways. Maurin's and Day's goal was to distribute the paper from public squares, sell it on street corners, and hand it out in front of meeting halls. The first issue was distributed during a protest in Union Square in New York City on May 1, 1933. The paper's circulation grew rapidly during the years of the Great Depression. Within one year, the readership increased from 2,500 to 35,000. Interest in the paper peaked during the worst years of the Great Depression. The circulation climbed to 150,000 in the first two years[2] but later declined significantly when it took an unpopular and difficult pacifist stance regarding World War II.

Finding adequate financial support to fund the paper was an issue from the very beginning. But neither Maurin nor Day allowed questions about how to fund the paper to halt or stall their efforts. Both Maurin and Day adopted the "God will provide" approach to budgeting. They devoted their own financial resources to pay for the paper and sold each copy for just a penny so that anyone could afford to buy the *Catholic Worker*. (The price of the paper has never changed.) Over time, supporters of the paper urged Dorothy to begin to look at the venture as a business. She reflected, "But this isn't a business, it's a movement. And we don't know anything about business here anyway."[3]

The Catholic Worker Movement from its very beginning was a movement of laypeople. The movement's origin among the laity contrasts with some other movements for social reform in the twentieth century, such as the primarily Protestant Social Gospel. Most historians characterize the Social Gospel as a movement founded and advanced primarily by clergy—Washington Gladden, Frank Mason North, and Walter Rauschenbusch. Revisionist histories emphasize some notable exceptions, including lay leaders such as Jane Addams, Vida Dutton Scudder, and Nannie Helen Burroughs. The Catholic Worker Movement was led by laity, even though some of their most loyal supporters and benefactors were members of religious orders. Some of the greatest support came from Sister Peter Claver, one of the first donors, and authors who sent both their writing and financial support, including Daniel and Philip Berrigan and Trappist monk Thomas Merton.

Communicating the Vision

In addition to editing the paper, Dorothy authored a regular column. The column appeared under different titles, beginning under the title of "The Listener" in 1933, later under the titles of "Day by Day" and "Day after Day," and then finally transitioning in 1946 to "On Pilgrimage." Her column combined reportage of significant events at the Catholic Worker "headquarters" and house of hospitality and national and global concerns with sometimes very personal reflections. News about the needs of workers was juxtaposed with stories about the celebration of Tamar's birthday.

Readers must have felt like they knew Day through her regular column. She wrote about every aspect of Worker life—introducing deep theological and philosophical ideas, the exhausting and gratifying work of child rearing, the ups and down of communal living. Some of the content from her columns was later published in book form or integrated into her own autobiographical works. All of her books use a variety of forms of writing, including personal narrative, journal entry, religious essay, meditation, biographical sketch, anecdote, and self-critical analysis.[4]

Good journalistic writing, "Easy Essays," and devotional pieces were not the only means by which the *Catholic Worker* communicated its understanding of the plight of the masses or its vision for a new society. Art played a key role in engaging the imagination of readers and reaching out to those who couldn't read. Two artists are particularly important to name, Ade Bethune and Fritz Eichenberg. Their artwork has become a symbol of the movement itself. Artwork could reach anyone, even the least educated person, and represented some of the most radical ideas conveyed in the paper.

Ade Bethune became aware of the *Catholic Worker* in 1933. As an immigrant from Belgium, she identified with the issues the paper raised but "found its appearance shabby."[5] She submitted a few black-and-white illustrations for consideration. Her artwork, a linocut of St. Joseph the Carpenter, first appeared in the March 1934 issue. Bethune's style was distinctively modern and gave the paper a fresh and relevant flair.

Art historians place Bethune within a larger liturgical arts movement. Bethune's style can be compared to folk art and promoted simplified, blocky images that reduced forms to their essential components. The subjects that she chose to represent were intended to connect with both city and country people and emphasized themes related to the Catholic Worker Movement—sacred work, racial equality, pacifism, and ordinary saints. In the paper, her artwork depicting historical figures was often placed adjacent to articles about contemporary life. These images invited people who picked up the paper to respond in a deeper way to the relevance of Christian thought, tradition, and practice to contemporary social, economic, and political problems.

Bethune intentionally contrasted the machine-made and mass-produced images being produced at the time. Realistic and highly sentimental pictures of saints were extremely popular among Catholics. You will probably be familiar with late nineteenth- and early twentieth-century depictions of saints sitting in a prayerful position, hands clasped together, heads lifted up toward the clouds, and faces highlighted by rays of light streaming down from heaven. Bethune considered these machine-made images products of a consumer-driven society. Her saints were also workers. They worked while they prayed. Ora et labora. Their hands were getting dirty as their minds and hearts were turned to God. The first linocut of Joseph that she created for the *Catholic Worker* depicted the saint at work. Joseph, a carpenter, is standing behind and bending over a table as he works at his craft with a chisel in hand. His sleeves are rolled up to the elbow, exposing his muscle. We can imagine the sweat dripping from his brow. This image of Joseph and her other pieces of artwork offered an alternative vision of saintliness and an image of a new society.

Fritz Eichenberg is another artist whose work significantly shaped the movement. He met Day in 1949 at a conference at Pendle Hill, a Quaker retreat center. Eichenberg's name betrays his German heritage. He was born in Cologne in 1901 to parents of Jewish background. The school he attended prepared young male students to fulfill their role as soldiers for the kingdom of Prussia. Very little emphasis was placed on the arts. The years leading up to and during the First World War were formative for Eichenberg. His experience of war and famine informed his social consciousness and pacifism throughout the rest of his life.

He, like so many others in his city, experienced hunger as their country invested so much in military operations. As a young adult, Eichenberg served as an artist's apprentice and then worked as an artist-reporter and political cartoonist. Before Adolf Hitler rose to power, he was frequently the subject of Eichenberg's political cartoons. When it became clear that Hitler would become president, Eichenberg decided to leave Germany. In 1933 he traveled to Guatemala, from there to Mexico, and then through Texas, finally landing in New York. New York was the most attractive location for Eichenberg to settle. He returned to Germany to retrieve his family.

In the United States, Eichenberg became a book illustrator and illustrated, among other books, Dostoyevsky's *Crime and Punishment*. He became a Quaker in 1940 and was attracted to the Quaker belief that Christ could be present in all people, and he appreciated their emphasis on spiritual equality. When he met Day at Pendle Hill she asked him to do some illustrations for the *Catholic Worker*.

Eichenberg thought of "art as a sacrament." His black-and-white illustrations, many of them reminiscent of the style of Albrecht Dürer (a master and artist of the sixteenth century Protestant movement for reform), captured the spirit of the movement. Saints Vincent de Paul and Anthony were the first two illustrations he created at Day's request. Over several decades he created drawings and engravings of saints or prophets from the past such as Mary, Joseph, Martin de Porres, Francis of Assisi, and Erasmus. More contemporary leaders were also the subjects of his artwork, including Gandhi, Martin Buber, Cesar Chavez, Thomas Merton, and Peter Maurin. Some of his best-known illustrations are woodcuts: "Christ of the Breadlines" (1953) and "The Lord's Supper" (1953). In "Christ of the Breadlines," Jesus appears standing in a line of homeless people waiting to be fed. "The Lord's Supper" depicts Jesus eating at the table of the Catholic Worker house. Eichenberg's artwork provided a window into the soul of the movement itself.

A Tool to Raise Consciousness about Poverty and the Plight of Workers

Papers, journals, serials, and novels in the first half of the twentieth century were critical tools used to raise public consciousness concerning wealth inequalities, the mistreatment of workers, social attitudes toward immigrants, and the need to provide for "adequate subsistence" for families. One example is Upton Sinclair's book *The Jungle*, which was first published in serial form in socialist newspapers. Many religious social activists also used novels or plays to spread their ideas for reform and highlight injustices. Charles Sheldon, a Congregationalist pastor, began serving as editor of the Topeka *Daily Capital* in 1900 and vowed to edit the paper according to Christian principles. Sheldon is probably best known for his novel *In His Steps or What Would Jesus Do?* that was also first published in serial form in the *Advance*, a small church newspaper in Chicago.

The *Catholic Worker* was designed to raise consciousness about the church's social mission, expose systemic and structural injustices, and appeal to workers who were being exploited by the industries they served. The first edition of

the paper, distributed on May 1, 1933, included a story that examined the poor working conditions for women garment workers. A letter to the editor reported that women were being paid meager wages of "8 cents a dozen" for "twenty-four seams." Later issues published statistics and data concerning the stark realities of income inequalities during the Great Depression.

The importance of the *Catholic Worker* in reporting information on wealth inequalities needs to be considered in context. An official federal definition of poverty was not adopted in the United States until 1969. There were a number of "unofficial poverty lines" that emerged in the United States before economist and statistician Mollie Orshansky developed poverty thresholds. The concept of poverty lines came out of a larger "social process." Economist Gordon Fisher observes that "[e]arly U.S. poverty lines grew out of a conflict during the late nineteenth and early twentieth century between two social groups with sharply opposed interests—urban industrial workers (many of them immigrants from southern and eastern Europe) and their families, and factory owners and industrialists who often violently resisted paying the workers a living wage."[6] The data that the *Catholic Worker* reported on the wealth divide should be viewed as an essential effort made within a larger movement of religious social activists and other advocates.

Raising Consciousness about Racism as a "Stupid Sin"

The *Catholic Worker* paper showed a progressive approach to advocacy early on by connecting economic injustices to racial discrimination. One of the issues addressed in the first edition of the paper was "The Negro in Labor," which discussed the plight of sharecroppers in the South. The language used to refer to the African American workers shows the influence of the era, but the editors were clear from the beginning that they did not want the *Catholic Worker* to be just "a white paper."[7] Appeals were made as early as 1934 for African Americans to contribute articles about their lived experience of race hatred and discrimination.

Reporting about lynching was particularly important in the 1930s. There was an upsurge in lynching at that time, likely related to the economic circumstances of the Great Depression. Day told the story of Iola Ellis in the article "Valiant is the Word" that was printed in March 1938. Ellis was a well-educated woman who became supervisor of the "colored schools" in Memphis, Tennessee. She and her husband witnessed a lynching in Memphis. The *Catholic Worker* made sure to report Ellis's experience in her own words.

> "They cut off the head of the poor dead body and dragged it down Beale Street. . . . The fingers and

toes were displayed in the windows of shops. That was in 1923. My husband could not stand it. He could not stand the sight of a white man for a while. The horror was too much for him."[8]

The fear, indignation, and disgust that Ellis and her family felt forced them to move north to Cleveland, Ohio. Ellis was discriminated against in the north too. The only job that she could get in Cleveland was "pushing a mop at a police station." Ellis's family faced other obstacles. Her nieces were barred from attending many white high schools. A bishop finally came to their aid and found placements for Ellis's nieces in Catholic schools. Day questioned how many Catholic schools were open to African Americans. In the article, she highlighted the growing numbers of African Americans within the membership of the Communist Party and called for the church to cultivate a new generation of black Catholic leaders.

It is worth making the observation here that some of the other movements for economic justice among Christian social activist groups have been criticized by contemporary theologians and ethicists for not identifying the relationship of race to economic injustice. While there were some exceptions among white women social gospelers, white male leaders such as Washington Gladden, Walter Rauschenbusch, and Shailer Mathews did not make raising consciousness about race hatred a priority or central to the mission of the Social Gospel movement. Contemporary scholars suggest that the black social gospel identified with Ida B. Wells-Barnett and Reverdy C. Ransom should be considered separately.

The *Catholic Worker* was clear from the beginning that racism could not be ignored when addressing the root causes of poverty and alternative Christian visions for society. The *Catholic Worker* recorded interviews with and stories of black people who had been discriminated against. Articles and editorials in the paper confronted head on unjust laws such as the Jim Crow laws in the South, which enforced a vicious system of racial segregation between 1877 and 1954. The stories of black men and women who had been tortured and executed by lynching were remembered by eyewitnesses when the dominant white media continued to present these issues in racist ways.

Christ Rooms

In its first six months, the *Catholic Worker* had only been a paper. But then winter hit New York, and people living on the streets began to knock on the door of Day's East 15th Street apartment in search of shelter. Day and Maurin knew that they had to put their ideas into practice as need arose. The concept for the house of hospitality was based on the notion of a city of hospitality developed by two theologians of the early church, Basil the Great and Jerome. Maurin believed that traditions of hospitality should be revived in parishes and in the homes of people of faith.

Basil, the brother of Gregory of Nyssa, founded a city of hospitality in Cappadocia in the fourth century. He believed that the "coat that hangs in the closet belongs to the poor." In other words, everything that you own that is in excess of what you need to satisfy the basic necessities of life does not actually belong to you but to those who are truly poor, those who have nothing. Maurin believed that Basil's city of hospitality could be recreated on a smaller scale if Christian families designated a space in their own home as a "Christ room" open to any who might have need. It was Jerome who first used the language of "Christ room."

Maurin and Day did not intend to create a new institution, a "Home" with a capital "H," to provide care for people who were homeless. Maurin favored having "a big pot on the stove and a continual supply of vegetable soup, constantly renewed from day to day."[9] Day's apartment became the first hospitality house. She opened the door to welcome people off the street to eat at her table and to sleep in any extra space possible. When it became clear that they needed more room, particularly for women requesting help, Day arranged to rent more apartments on E. 15th Street. The first one was named the "Teresa-Joseph Cooperative" in honor of both Teresa of Avila, the medieval woman mystic, and Joseph, Jesus' "foster father."

Day wrote about the women who lived at the Teresa-Joseph Cooperative in her "Day by Day" column of June 1, 1934, and then later included the same story in *The Long Loneliness*. The story underscored the importance of inclusion for residents of houses of hospitality. A woman whom Day described as a "colored woman" named Mary had come to the hospitality house to eat. Mary appeared to be "in need of a shelter where she could stay in bed and rest for a few days instead of having to walk the streets from morning to night as the guests of the [Municipal] lodging house have to do."[10] Day did not want "to run the risk of submitting her to insult on account of her color." She went to ask the other women staying there if it would be all right to invite Mary to stay. As she reflected on the event, Day mentioned that she did not expect too much from the women living there in terms of freedom from racial prejudice. "I talked to the girls," she wrote, "reminding them how our Lord washed the feet of his disciples the night before he suffered and died for us, and told them how we all should serve each other, whether we are white, black, or

yellow."[11] As Day told the story, the women welcomed Mary without hesitation.

The Inefficiency of Hospitality

In 1936, when money and other circumstances allowed, the headquarters of the Catholic Worker moved from Day's apartment to 115 Mott Street and, in that same year, thirty-three Catholic Worker houses were founded across the country. Day's book about the beginnings of the Catholic Worker, *House of Hospitality,* captures a glimpse of what life would have been like in a Worker house at the beginning of the movement. She wrote that "minutes and hours and days were taken up doing everything else in the world except getting out a paper and answering letters in connection with that paper."[12] Much of Day's daily routine was taken up with mundane tasks of getting food for staff and visitors, cleaning up from meals without the help of dishwashing machines, taking out garbage, cleaning toilets, settling disputes between residents in the houses, getting ready for educational sessions, doling out clothes that had been donated, and the like.

Living in a house of hospitality was like living with a large family. People came to stay there for an indefinite length of time. Some were attracted to the house because they needed shelter. Others were attracted because they wanted to work for the paper, to voluntarily choose poverty, and/or to live in community. They wanted to be part of a movement. Most of the people who came to work for the paper were also required to take on other jobs. Editors for the paper became cooks. The circulation manager served as dishwasher.

There were no rules any more than a family has rules. In fact, this created some problems, primarily with authority in the community. If everyone coming there was part of the family, then who had the right to determine how people would conduct themselves in the home? An individual worker trying to impose specific rules on others would receive a quick reprimand from Day. John Cort, a Catholic convert and socialist who became a Worker, told the story of his experience in this way: "The notion was that, according to personalism, or personal responsibility as it was called, you didn't tell people anything. You just set a good example and hoped they'd profit from your good example and begin to do good things."[13] As we might imagine, this concept of exercising personal responsibility didn't always work too well. Cort remembered deciding to post some simple rules one day because people weren't helping around the house. Day told Cort to take them down. From Day's perspective, everyone entered on a level place. No one was asked any questions. People had to begin to do good things out of their own volition.

Fostering this sense of personal responsibility and allowing anyone to enter without asking questions would be an innovative practice even today for a house that offers temporary and long-term shelter to people who outsiders might call the "needy." In this practice, the Catholic Workers challenged a prevalent assumption and approach in the United States at that time about how to assist the "needy." In order to qualify for aid, people should first be distinguished in terms of "deserving" or "undeserving" of help. For example, people who lived in poverty could prove that they were "deserving" of aid if they could show that they had not remained "idle" and worked as much as possible to fulfill their own needs. The "undeserving" would be seen as victims of their own laziness and therefore not necessarily worthy of social assistance. Categorizing people as "deserving" or "undeserving" also reflected the dominant approach to the social and economic system. Individuals competed within a market-based economy to achieve their own aims and the market would determine their value based on the contribution that they made to production.

Valuing and Welcoming all Members of the Mystical Body of Christ

A Christian concept of hospitality prevented Catholic Workers from valuing people on the basis of their contribution to production. People entering the doors of a house of hospitality were valued simply because they were created in the image of God and shared a common nature and common needs. The house of hospitality modeled a way of living by an alternative social and economic reality. Day drew on Paul's theological concept of the mystical body of Christ as the basis for an essential relatedness of all people:

> For as in one body we have many members, and not
> all the members have the same function, so we, who
> are many, are one body in Christ, and individually we
> are members one of another. (Rom. 12:4–5)

If everyone is a member of the mystical body of Christ, then
making distinctions about helping others on the basis of
whether people could be determined as "deserving" or
"undeserving" according to society's standards becomes
pointless and irrelevant. Day wrote, "St. Paul says 'When
the health of one member of the Mystical body suffers, the
health of the whole body is lowered.'"[14]

Dorothy connected the mystical body of Christ with the
essential relatedness of all people and the circumstances of
people living in poverty in her society. The concept of the
mystical body of Christ placed workers in the context of a
different economy, a divine economy, in which they are
valued equally as an essential part of the whole body. It is
worth mentioning that Day's interpretation of the body
seems to differ somewhat from the notion of the Mystical
Body of Christ described in the official doctrine of the
Catholic Church. In 1943, four years after *House of Hospitality* was published, Pope Pius XII wrote the encyclical
Mystici Corporis Christi. In Pius's encyclical, the "body of
Christ" and the "Church" are the same. For Day, the purpose of the Catholic Worker was to illumine the mystical
body of Christ in the people on the street. She connected
the body of Christ to the other.

Hospitality houses embraced ecumenism and multicul-
turalism as part of their identity. Catholic Workers collaborated with and reached out to Jews, Protestants, and
Catholics, among others. This approach may not seem
novel in the twenty-first century, but it was innovative in
the broader context of ecumenical and interfaith work in
the mid-to-late 1930s. Modern ecumenism as it developed

in an institutionalized form in the late nineteenth and early twentieth century began in Protestant communities and circles. Establishing ecumenical organizations was an important effort to transcend the divisions between Protestant denominations. The Federal Council of Churches (FCC), one of the most important national ecumenical organizations in the early twentieth century and precursor to the National Council of Churches, was founded in 1908.

The Catholic Church resisted on an official level the ecumenical spirit exhibited by Protestant communities. In his encyclical *Mortalium Animos* (1928), Pope Pius XI warned against modern ideas that could lead to compromises with Catholic doctrine and spoke against an understanding of the church that would allow it to be seen as an organization composed of independent bodies holding different beliefs. The Catholic Worker Movement represents an instance of a movement that emerged from the laity and embodied on a personal level a Catholic spirit of ecumenical and interfaith cooperation. A letter to the editor written by John C. Paisley attests to the interest and inclusion that Protestants felt in the Catholic Worker Movement as well: "Although I am a Protestant, I prize your paper highly, because it gives good evidence that there is no excuse for ill feeling between Catholics and Protestants."[15] Many Protestants took a strong interest in and allied themselves with the Catholic Worker Movement.

The Catholic Worker communities consistently tried to live up to the ideal of hospitality as welcoming all. Catholic Worker communities were multicultural. Many people who were part of the community with whom Dorothy lived and/or attended its programs were immigrants—French, Irish, Polish, Lithuanian, Italian, Ukrainian, Spanish, German, Belgian, and Armenian. Catholic Worker communities today still reflect this multicultural identity.

Outsiders to the Catholic Worker community, particularly city officials, did not understand what they were trying to accomplish. Day observed:

> We were not running a restaurant or a lodging house, we explained. We were a group of individuals exercising personal responsibility in caring for those who came to us. They were not strangers, we point out, since we regarded them as brothers in Christ. We were not an institution or a Home with a capital letter, but a home, a private home.[16]

City officials in New York tried on several occasions to force the Catholic Workers to live up to rules defined for soup kitchens, lodging houses, or other charitable organizations.

Farming Communes

Farming communes were the third aspect of the "program of action." Maurin thought that capitalism and communism shared at least one problem in common: emerging from urban roots, both philosophies were disconnected from the land. He advocated for a "Green Revolution" that would be characterized by people coming together "to work out in a practical way an ethical economic system based on respect for the land."[17] Maurin thought that any real vision for a new economy should focus on the decentralization of industry and the reintroduction of small-scale agriculture as the means to help people living in poverty in urban centers. Farming communes bore the potential to return to a land-and-craft society. No unemployment could exist on a farm. There was always plenty of work for all.

Farming communes would emphasize the importance of "spiritually binding" the community of workers. Members

of the commune would have to recognize that their work was not only a partnership between themselves but also a partnership held between themselves, God, and the land. One of his "Easy Essays" illustrates this point:

> To work on a farming commune
> is to cooperate with God
> in the production of food.

Subsistence farming was the model adopted for the farm's production of food. Maurin underscored the importance of eating, not selling, the food that they produced.

Retreating from Urban Life

The Catholic Workers began experimenting with farming communes in 1935 after renting a house on Staten Island. Day referred to the first farm as a "garden commune" because of its small size. In April 1936, the same year that the headquarters was established at 115 Mott Street, they purchased a thirty-acre farm in Easton, Pennsylvania. She named the farm in Easton "Maryfarm." The basic organization for the farm was taken from a Benedictine monastic model. A group of families lived off the land, shared daily Mass, prayed, studied, and labored together, and subjected themselves to one another and "the benign authority of an abbot-like coordinator."[18]

Day understood the importance of retreating from urban life. She took many trips to and from the city to the farm during the year that it was being established. During the summer, her daughter, Tamar, also benefitted from living in the environment outside the city. Day and other workers living on the farm were required to learn new types of work to keep the farm going. Day's work extended beyond writing, cooking, cleaning, and canning to herding cows. Tamar met her husband, David Hennessy, while living at the Worker farm and, after they married, the young couple tried to live the ideal worker life on the farm. It proved to be difficult.

Many of the people who were attracted to living on the farm were often interested because of theological or political reasons. They were intrigued by the concept of agronomic universities more than by manual labor. Few of them had much experience in farming. Sometimes they did not work sufficiently hard to provide enough food to sustain the community, making food scarce. In Day's biography of Maurin, she remembered a summer when Peter decided not to eat eggs or to drink milk. He had witnessed an argument between two members of the community because one of them ate an egg another had set aside for lunch.

Other disagreements developed with regard to authority within the farming commune. Maryfarm was open as a farm commune for only a few years because of a dispute that developed among the workers there. The men in the upper farm began to consider themselves the "true Catholic Workers" and ruled their households with an insistence on the strict obedience of women. In 1947, the farm in Easton was sold. The upper farm was deeded to the "true Catholic Workers." The lower farm was sold to local people. Soon after the end of WWII, Maryfarm became a retreat center for Workers. Subsequent farms were established in Newburgh (1947) and then on Staten Island (1950). The farm on Staten Island was named the "Maurin Farm." Later the farm was moved to a location on the Hudson River after a mansion and outbuildings were purchased in 1964. There the farm was known as Tivoli. Rosalie Riegle said that Tivoli became "a haven for wandering hippies, men from the road, idealists seeking utopian community, and Dorothy's aging friends."[19]

Spiritual Practices Sustaining the Movement

While Day's description of life in a hospitality house sounds conducive to just about anything but contemplation, she begins the book she wrote about her first experiences in this environment with a kind of orientation to the contemplative life. The first chapter of *House of Hospitality* begins with the story of Pythagoras dividing the days of his disciples into three parts. One third of the day would be spent for God in prayer. A second third of the day would be spent for God in study and meditation. And the last third of the day would be devoted to the care of human beings and focused on the business of life. Day admitted that caregiving responsibilities prevented her from following Pythagoras's pattern exactly, but she clearly identified the importance of contemplation and meditation in the midst of all of her activities.

Day attended Mass daily and developed her own daily spiritual practices, including reading the Psalms, prayer, and manual labor. Workers were encouraged to worship and attend Mass regularly in local parishes near the house of hospitality in which they lived. Maurin drafted a schedule that he hoped to be used by the farming communes. The schedule was based on the monastic model and patterned the day according to the rhythm of work and prayer. While neither the hospitality houses nor the farming communes strictly followed a schedule, they did maintain a daily regimen. Day visited a farming commune called the Grail that was located in Foster, Ohio, in May 1943 and took note of their daily schedule in her diary. Their schedule included a combination of formal prayer, Mass, time reserved for meditation, and manual labor.

Scholars and religious leaders commenting about the importance of Day's spirituality in her work often point to her support for the liturgical movement and experience of retreats. Rooted in the work of Benedictine Virgil Michel, the liturgical movement sought to renew the Roman Catholic Church's emphasis on Scripture and the sacrament. Day nurtured a lasting friendship with Fr. Michel and felt a strong connection to the movement he inspired. She underscored the significance of the movement for Catholic Workers: "We feel that it is very necessary to connect the liturgical movement with the social justice movement. Each one gives vitality to the other."[20]

Michel sought to revive an understanding of the Pauline concept of the body of Christ as a living organism. He understood the liturgy as an act of worship connected to daily life. On one level, Michel's understanding of the liturgy challenged the materialism, individualism, and indifference pervading society in the United States. "Indeed, the body does not consist of one member but of many" (1 Cor. 12:14). On another level, the liturgical movement challenged a tendency in Catholic theology before the Second

Vatican Council to relegate religion to "the privacy of one's home with curtains drawn." For Michel, participating in the liturgy and receiving the sacrament was a way of orienting one's nature and actions toward the transcendent. Michel visited with the Workers and prayed the Compline, which is an evening prayer that invites reflection on the day's events. After their experience of the nightly examination of conscience, the practice became a custom during evenings at Worker houses. It is the connection between the life of prayer, mysticism, and social action to which we now turn our attention in the next chapter. Social mysticism enabled Day to bring together two loyalties—loyalty to the Workers and loyalty to the church—and to harness them for a common cause.

CHAPTER FOUR

A Social Mystic

We may wonder how and why Dorothy Day was able to open herself up to such vulnerability in the world, in her relationships with friends and family, and even in the church. For most of us, her choices seem to defy social conventions, logic, reason, and practicality. Even though it was difficult, Day walked away from the love and familiarity that she knew in her relationship with Forster and risked the vulnerability that would be part of a life lived as a single mother in the 1930s. Many of her close friends and family, who devoted themselves to socialist causes, did not understand her religiosity. For them, religious belief was a delusion. Day, however, was unable to resist the persistent feeling that there was more to the world than what was evident to the naked eye. Eventually Day became a highly regarded lay social activist in the Roman Catholic Church. This could not have been an easy undertaking, particularly for a woman in the pre-Vatican II Roman Catholic community.

These actions and deliberate choices cannot be understood apart from the anchoring of her activities in a ritual of daily prayer and mystical experiences. Social mysticism enabled Day to navigate the deep and turbulent waters between her opposition to capitalism and her commitment to the anticommunist Catholic Church. Day encountered the divine in the midst of her daily activities. She came to recognize that her social activities were not just an end in themselves but the expression of her resistance to social and political artifices that created false boundaries between human beings, God, and the natural world.

Day drew on the insights of mystical writers, fueled her work with prayer and routine spiritual practices, and steadied herself in dynamic relationship with the divine as she faced head-on the depth of the world's chaos and disorder. Many of her models and mentors of mystical experience were people from the past who saw the deep connection between mysticism and social passion. Day discovered the linkages between the contemplative life and social action. She developed a heightened consciousness of the sacredness of all things through the writings of theologians and mystics such as Augustine of Hippo, Catherine of Siena, Thomas à Kempis, Teresa of Avila, and Thérèse of Lisieux.

Theologies that emerge from mystical experiences are not neatly defined and well-organized theories. We will not be investigating the development of Day's social mysticism in a predictably chronological or rigidly systematic way. The pages that follow situate Day's social mysticism in a larger tradition of mysticism in Western Christianity and describe Day's own distinctive expression of social mysticism.

Mysticism within a Larger Tradition of Christianity

When trying to understand Day's expression of social mysticism, it is important to situate social mysticism within a larger tradition of Christian mysticism and attend to different approaches to the connection between mysticism and social concern. Theologian Bradley Holt points out that the term mysticism itself is "elastic, used by different writers in different ways."[1] Mysticism refers to a form of spirituality that sees the complete union of body, mind, and spirit with God or the gods as its ultimate goal. A mystic is someone who has a direct intuitive encounter with a reality that transcends human experience. The response of the mystic to the divine is intensely personal and invites one to center all aspects of one's own reality in relation to and for relationship with God.

Ursula King, an expert in the study of Christian spirituality, says that Christian mysticism began during the second century of our common era. Early mysticism was shaped by the experiences of ascetics and monks who had been influenced by two theologians in the early church, Clement of Alexandria and Origen. As a tradition of mysticism in Western Christianity began to solidify and develop, Gregory of Nyssa, Augustine of Hippo, and Dionysius the Areopagite emerged as three of the most important figures writing about their own experiences of God.

King observes that Gregory of Nyssa's writings provide "abundant proof that mysticism is not something apart from life and the concerns of the world."[2] Gregory was part of a remarkable family from the province of

Cappadocia in Asia Minor. His sister, Macrina, turned much of her family's vast wealth into social ministries. Gregory, who recorded her story, thought of her as an example of the Christian life. Macrina persuaded another brother, Basil, to give up his career as a scholar to become a monk. Basil is especially noted for turning his monastery into a social service institution. Remember that Basil's city of hospitality served as a model for the house of hospitality founded by Day and Maurin.

Augustine's *Confessions* (dated between 397–398 CE) remains one of the most widely read Christian spiritual autobiographies even in the present day. Whether or not the label *mystic* accurately defines him, the evidence of mysticism in the *Confessions* is unmistakable. Augustine wrote about the travail and transitions that characterized his own past and traced how God had been seeking him throughout his life. He was born in Tagaste and moved to different cities to seek an education and then to work. When he finally returned to Tagaste permanently he formed a contemplative community and committed himself to it during the remainder of his life.

The word mysticism made its way into Christian theology through the writing of Pseudo-Dionysius. *Theologia Mystica* describes the importance of leaving behind the senses and operations of the intellect in order to be united with God. Dionysius denied that one could know God through the power of the intellect. Rather, one knows God in a state of utter passivity that "leads to an ecstasy of love in which the human is fused with God."[3]

Most mystics in the early Christian church were contemplatives; that is, they lived a life of prayer. The connection between mysticism, the life patterned by an intentional practice of prayer, and social action is not always clearly understood. In fact, mysticism is often misunderstood and mischaracterized as a direct encounter with the divine that leads only to a life of isolation. Even a brief introduction to the beginnings of mysticism in Western Christianity alludes to some ways Christians in the early church connected mysticism to social concern. In the twentieth century, the concern to connect mysticism and work for social transformation bore a heightened sense of importance for many Christian activists who were trying to reconcile Christian practice and belief with new scientific discoveries, technological advances in industry and warfare, and accelerating wealth inequalities, among other things.

Three Approaches to the Question of Mysticism and Social Concern

Vida Dutton Scudder, an Anglican lay leader and social gospeler, observed that mysticism was being revived in the twentieth century through the writings of popular authors such as Evelyn Underhill and Rufus Jones. Many churches were intentionally cultivating an interest in mysticism among their members by sponsoring discussion groups related to it. In August 1939, Day and Scudder both attended and served as leadership for a conference on the "Main Currents of Christian Social Thought and Action Today." The conference was held in South Byfield, Massachusetts, at Adelynrood, the retreat center of the Society of Companions of the Holy Cross (SCHC). The SCHC was an organization of Episcopal lay women who did not live in cloistered settings but banded together to pray for concerns of the modern world. Scudder, a member of the SCHC, introduced the hopes for the two-day conference and concluded the conversation at the end of the second day. Day spoke on "The Catholic Worker and Its Enterprises." Meditation, prayer, and communion set the tone and rhythm of each day while lectures and discussion groups focused on "Social Theory and Practice in the Roman Catholic Church," "Roman Catholic Social Experiments," and "Protestant Theory and Social Practice."[4]

Earlier that same year, Scudder published an article in *The World Tomorrow* on "Mysticism and Social Passion" that referred to a rich debate among theologians and activists about the relevance of mysticism, not as a form of retreat, but rather as a form of resistance to the dehumanizing aspects of modern life. The way in which Scudder framed this debate informs our examination of three approaches to the connection between mysticism and social concern and the description of Day as a "social mystic."

The first two approaches share in common the notion that making a strong connection between mysticism and social concern is problematic. A *mysticism of detachment,* the first approach, emphasizes that the fulfillment of the mystical experience and union with God is found in total detachment from the world. Material things, including the body itself, are seen as a distraction from one's relationship with God. In contrast, the second approach, a *rejection of mysticism,* criticizes forms of mysticism that lead to isolation from the world and underscores the rigorous engagement of the intellect as a sign of obedience to God. The third approach, *social mysticism,* sees mysticism and social passion as helpless without each other. Social mysticism, in my opinion, best describes the way in which Day rooted her activism in a life of prayer and encounters with the divine in the midst of her daily activities.

The *mysticism of detachment* is based on the understanding that God is self-sufficient in Godself and wholly other than the world. God resides in the heavens and acts on the earth only at God's own choosing. Human beings become one with God by fighting against and overcoming their own

bodily needs and desires. God does not reside in material things; therefore union with God is found in total detachment from them. Platonism of the second century offers an example of the mysticism of detachment as it developed from a notion that human beings were essentially spiritual in nature. The journey of the soul is to return to and seek union with God. The sermons of Meister Eckhart provide another example as he emphasized the fulfillment of the mystic within the inner life. Theologian, pastor, and civil rights leader Howard Thurman described Eckhart's understanding of mysticism in this way:

> [T]his form of mysticism is one of obedience and confidence. In the image of Eckhardt (sic), there is an uncreated element in the soul of the individual. It is

> such an insight that declares that it is possible for the individual to touch a divinely-formed point of contact with God within his own soul. As Eckhardt (sic) puts it: the uncreated element, the given element, in the soul of man is in his language the very God.[5]

Theologians, both past and present, have been troubled by the understanding of God and the spiritual practices that support a mysticism of detachment. God is defined almost exclusively in terms of transcendence (independence from and wholly other than human beings and the world) with little or no emphasis on God's immanence (existence within and among human beings and the world). Thurman himself took issue with Eckhart's understanding in that it recognized "the primary experience of God with the personal core of the individual."[6] Neither the connection of God with the world nor the interdependence of body and spirit are honored. From this perspective, social concern and the fulfillment of bodily desires become a distraction from or impediment to union with God. While mysticism understood in this way may not be intended as a direct attack on the work of social justice, a mysticism of detachment does not concern itself with satisfying bodily needs and tends to view overcoming one's desire to satisfy one's own bodily needs and desires as evidence of a higher calling.

Some theologians in the twentieth century argued that such an approach to the Christian life supports an understanding of the mission of the church that focuses on spiritual ideals at the expense of addressing the concrete needs of people living in poverty. Walter Rauschenbusch, one of the best-known social gospel theologians of that time and a friend of Scudder's, rejected forms of mysticism that placed too strong an emphasis on individual, affective experiences of God. "Its danger is that it isolates. In energetic mysticism the soul concentrates on God, shuts out the world, and is conscious only of God and itself."[7] Social, economic, and political structures and systems that create poverty too often remain unchallenged.

Rejection of Mysticism

Many other Christians rejected mysticism because they believed that it leads only toward detachment from the rest of the world. Christians who identify with Reformed traditions—Presbyterians, United Church of Christ, the Reformed Church of America, Christian Reformed, etc.—have been prone to reject mysticism, instead emphasizing the centrality of the "Word" and seeking union with God through the rigorous exercise of the intellect. From this perspective, God is still often seen as an otherworldly reality, self-sufficient in Godself. However, God is also understood to be concerned about human realities, particularly human frailties. God desires reconciliation with God and among human beings. Jesus Christ is the historical example of God bridging the gap between God and humanity. The centrality of the "Word," most frequently interpreted as the biblical text, is a distinctive mark of Reformed theologies. Rigorous engagement with and seeking to follow the "Word" is the way in which faithful people show gratitude to God for God's action and work to place God at the center of all values. Reformed Christians often approach "spirituality" and mystical experiences with suspicion.

Martin Luther, a sixteenth-century reformer, referred to mystical theology as "twaddle" and condemned mysticism for being more Platonic than Christian. Reformed theologian Reinhold Niebuhr, recognized by many as one of the United States' most notable public theologians of the twentieth century, argued that history and all the struggles for love and justice were in danger of being "swallowed up by eternity" in the mystical experience. Mystics understood well "the transcendent freedom of the human spirit; but . . . [did] not understand it in its organic relations to the temporal process."[8] Although this is changing somewhat in the twenty-first century, Reformed Christians historically have tended to discount the importance of the emotional or affective religious experience.

Social Mysticism and Dorothy Day

Neither of the first two approaches to mysticism and its connection to social concern defines well Day's experiences or writings. The *mysticism of detachment* and the *rejection of mysticism* also fail to take seriously the many examples of mystics who, because of their direct intuitive experience of God, were led to immerse themselves deeply into the world's troubled waters. Early academic studies of mysticism focused more on the psychological dimensions of mysticism than the connection between mysticism and social concern. Studies that have developed in recent years are making stronger connections between mysticism and prophetic cries for justice. *Social mysticism* represents a third alternative in which mysticism and social passion are seen as helpless without each other. As a social mystic, Day developed a kind of "double vision" that enabled her to experience the divine in the pursuit of a social aim. She wrote,

> [Christ] is with us in our kitchens, at our tables, on our breadlines, with our visitors, on our farms. When we pray for our material needs, it brings us close to His humanity. He, too, needed food and shelter. He too, warmed His hands at a fire and lay down in a boat to sleep. When we have spiritual reading at meals, when we have the rosary at night, when we

have study groups, forums, when we go out to distribute literature at meetings, or sell it on street corners, Christ is there with us.[9]

In Western Christianity, and, more specifically for Roman Catholics, many mystics have cultivated a "double vision" by living a life patterned by prayer.

This certainly was true for Day. She began regularly attending Mass even when she was living with Forster. The house of hospitality that she and Maurin developed adopted many of the spiritual practices associated with monastic life. Day herself practiced her own daily rule, participated in spiritual retreats, and planned them for those who became part of the Catholic Worker community. She lived in a cloistered monastic community only for a brief time when she took a leave of absence from the Catholic Worker community but never felt comfortable in a cloistered environment. Day learned to meditate "here, there, and everywhere—at the kitchen table, on the train, on the ferry, on my way to

and from appointments and even while making supper or putting Teresa [Tamar] to bed."[10] Cultivating a life of prayer did not lead her to remove herself from others, but it did open her up to interpreting her relationship with others differently.

Howard Thurman's lecture "Mysticism and Social Action" provides powerful insights that are useful for deepening our understanding of Day's social mysticism. He wrote, "[T]he mystic's concern with the imperative of social action is not merely to improve the condition of society. . . . For the mystic, social action is sacramental because it is *not* an end in itself."[11] In the context of industrialization in the twentieth century, social action then can be seen as the means by which one resists forces that dehumanize, depersonalize, and disintegrate one's awareness of the interdependence of neighbor, God, and nature.

Day's Writings as Spiritual Autobiography

Writing was one of Day's primary activities. All of her work contains elements of her own experience. In chapter 1, we explored two of Day's autobiographies, *The Long Loneliness* and *From Union Square to Rome*. Neither of these books concentrates on Day's development in chronological terms. Her autobiographies express Day's own understanding of the way in which she encountered God in different people, places, and events and how she came to discover that God had been seeking her throughout her life. In this way, her autobiographies and some of her other works can be compared to the writing of Augustine.

Augustine introduced a narrative character into early Christian writing. His most celebrated book, the *Confessions,* reconstructed past events in his life to show that God had been searching for him throughout his life. Day also quoted Augustine many times in her diaries, often using his writings to reflect on or interpret her own experiences. In an entry dated February 1944 she wrote, "The sins of my entire past life from earliest childhood come often to my mind to fill me with a sense of iniquity. St. Augustine was right when he talked of the wickedness there is even in children."[12] Later in her life she referred to Augustine's writings as a continued source of wisdom, "I began to feel old. I brooded on this for a day and suddenly while reading St. Augustine, had a marvelous sense of this truth that no matter how old one becomes there was always a possibility of an increase of knowledge, through books and people, and the world around us."[13]

Day Compared to Catherine of Siena

Peter Maurin compared Day to Catherine of Siena. In 1970 the Roman Catholic Church recognized Catherine as a saint and doctor of the church. Idealized biographies of the saints, also called hagiographies, will seem larger than life and sensational to most people today. However, hagiography as a genre or type of writing needs to be considered in light of its intent. The purpose of hagiography is to inspire readers by teaching how ordinary people can be seized by a sense of restlessness as they discover God's presence in the midst of the world and begin to express their experience of God through acts of healing. Saints are remembered for continuing Jesus' acts of healing in a similar way as the apostles in the book of Acts in the New Testament. Recall the passage in Acts: "Awe came upon everyone, because many wonders and signs were being done by the apostles" (Acts 2:43).

No one who reads the story of Catherine of Siena could avoid questioning its historical accuracy. Hagiographers describe Catherine's extreme asceticism, devotion to poverty, and care for the poor and sick. Catherine defies illness after she sucks the pus from the wounds of the sick. She survives most of her life by eating only bitter herbs and drinking water. Her bodily frame diminishes to the extent that she experiences visions and feels as if she loses herself in God's warm embrace. A comparison can be made here to Day's treatment of people living in poverty. Day once wrote about encountering a woman who was begging on the steps of a church in New York City. Cancer had eaten a gaping hole in the woman's face where her eye and nose had once been. The woman reached out to kiss Day's hand. Not feeling comfortable with the privilege implied by the woman's response the only thing that Day could think to do was to kiss the woman's face.[14]

Maurin likely compared Day to Catherine because of the way the saint's mystical experiences gave her authority in church and society and inspired her to become engaged in public affairs. Catherine's distinctive combination of faith and public action made her a popular saint and model for women in the twentieth century. She defied traditional norms of family in her time. Her mother and father wanted her to be married, but Catherine resisted. Catherine's encounters with God also gave her the authority and inspiration to become politically involved in the life of the church and broader society. The Roman Catholic Church was divided in her time. From 1309 to 1378 seven popes resided in Avignon, France. Catherine persuaded Pope Gregory XI to return the papacy to Rome from Avignon with the strength and clarity of her writing in her letters to him. Gregory XI was known for being excessively timid and hesitant to upset his cardinals. Maurin compared Dorothy to Catherine because her encounters with God led directly to acts of healing, political engagement, and advocacy on behalf of others.

Day Inspired by Saints of the Western and Eastern Churches

Day was inspired by the writings of both Western and Eastern Orthodox spiritual guides such as Teresa of Avila, Thérèse of Lisieux, Thomas à Kempis, and Elizabeth of Hungary and read their works alongside the work of popular socialist authors such as Jack London, Upton Sinclair, and Fyodor Dostoyevsky. She read these books not just once but returned to them again and again with questions about ways to address social and economic problems and in search of ways to deal with feelings of being a neglectful parent, physical and spiritual exhaustion, disillusionment, ineffectiveness, or anger.

Teresa of Avila influenced her greatly. Teresa was a Carmelite nun in Spain during the Spanish Inquisition. Most scholars today recognize that Teresa had a Jewish background and was influenced by both Christian and Jewish traditions, including those associated with Jewish kabbalistic mysticism, the Jesuits, and the Franciscans. Throughout her life Teresa reformed and founded convents for women all over Spain. She is also remembered for developing a concept of mental prayer associated with those who were persecuted by the Inquisition. Day quoted Teresa on many occasions: "Here our life is but a 'night spent in an uncomfortable inn,' as St. Teresa says." Day further reflected in her diary that she had learned from Teresa that God was in the midst of her life and the community as "my companion, friend, Lover—more my Master."[15]

Teresa's book *The Interior Castle* maintains a place as one of the classics of Western spirituality. The castle is an image of the soul wherein God takes God's delight. The castle contains seven mansions with many different rooms and the beginner enters by means of mental prayer and then travels through the different mansions, each of which represents a different stage of prayer life. The sixth mansion symbolizes the stage of spiritual betrothal to God. Spiritual marriage and full union with God are the discovery of the seventh mansion. Author David Scott observes that "[a]s she grew older, Day's writings on God and Christ became increasingly mystical and erotic, as she came to know God as spouse and lover."[16]

Thomas à Kempis's *Imitation of Christ* was one of Day's favorite books. On the surface, Kempis's book seems easily discounted as just a representative and remnant of medieval writing. Day, however, would have seen a social message at the heart of Kempis's book: One centers one's values in God by embodying Jesus' own passionate concern for others. Kempis himself was a member of a late-medieval spiritual movement called the *Devotio Moderna*. The movement was centered in Holland and defined its purpose to rekindle the enthusiasm and practical way of life practiced by the early Christian communities in Jerusalem. Members of the community, known as Brothers and Sisters of the Common Life, chose to live in voluntary poverty, chastity, and obedience either in their own homes or in community. They earned their living by the labor of their hands and their earnings were placed in a common fund.

Love and the "Little Way"

Social mysticism enabled Day to imagine an alternative way of living in the world and to challenge the capitalist approach to market economy. Social mysticism helped her to find a community where she could maintain a commitment both to her faith and her social conscience. Catholic Workers cannot be adequately understood apart from the social mysticism that fueled the theological, social, economic, and political imagination of the movement's founders. Day referred to the Catholic Workers' lifestyle, whether it was practiced in a hospitality house or in society, as the "little way." The "little way" is an expression found in the autobiographical writings of Thérèse of Lisieux.

Thérèse was a Carmelite nun who lived in a convent in Lisieux, France, and died of breast cancer at the age of twenty-four. Father Zachary, one of Day's confessors, gave her Thérèse's autobiography, *The Story of a Soul.* Dorothy felt patronized by the gift at first. She commented in her introduction to *Therese* that "Men, and priests too, were very insulting to women, I thought, handing out what they felt suited their intelligence; in other words, pious pap."[17] Thérèse's writings were popular during Day's lifetime but seemed highly sentimental, particularly at first reading. Ursula King describes Thérèse as

> a rather traditional woman, marked by that female obedience and dutiful submissiveness that were part of the nineteenth-century bourgeois expectations. Yet there was another tenacious and irrepressible side to her character, evident from her strong will and desire, impossible to realize, to be a missionary perhaps, or even a priest.[18]

Later, Day came to understand the social implications of Thérèse's writings. In *The Story of a Soul,* Thérèse felt conflicted as she was pulled by multiple commitments and vocations—"warrior, priest, apostle, doctor, and martyr."[19] What she ultimately discerns is that love itself comprises all vocations. She finds her place "in the Church. In the heart of the Church I shall be love. Thus everything, and thus my dream will be realized."[20] Her way of expressing that love she called the "little way."

Thérèse wrote about the "little way" as "a way of spiritual childhood," "the way of trust and surrender," "a way of confidence and total abandon," and taught that what people needed to do on earth was "to cast at Jesus the flowers of little sacrifices." The little way, however, could not just be understood as a way filled with "sweetness and consolation." For Thérèse, it was exactly the opposite. Thérèse thought that offering oneself in love meant to "offer one's self to suffering, because love lives only on sacrifice; so, if one is completely dedicated to loving, one must expect to be sacrificed unreservedly."[21] One's ability to love was strengthened through every act of resistance to self-will.

Thérèse also had a longing to "save sinners." For her, love was indistinguishable from her desire to save sinners. She defined sin in a somewhat distinctive way. She believed that the failure to experience God's love was just as much the motive for sin as the result of one's sin. Sinners in her society were often people who had been cast aside. Thérèse began to adopt social outcasts as her projects, including a man named Pranzini. Pranzini had been convicted of murdering a woman, her maid, and her child. Thérèse thought that she would be able to turn him around, transform him, through her prayers. Just before Pranzini was executed he grabbed a crucifix from the hand of a priest standing nearby and kissed Jesus' wounds. Thérèse thought of this as evidence of the effectiveness of her prayers. In this act, Thérèse believed that she and Pranzini now shared a bond a love. Love had overcome the artificial boundary established by society between them and brought Thérèse together with her neighbor.

Day underscored the social implications of Thérèse's writings in many of her own works, including articles she wrote for the *Catholic Worker* and in a book she published in 1960. What impressed Day the most was that Workers themselves insisted that Thérèse become a saint when she was being considered for canonization. Thérèse's teachings could be applied to the Catholic Worker Movement. Workers looked to walk her little way, her way of love. Each small act held significance—from washing dishes to editing the paper or from changing beds to participating in protests on behalf of workers. Even small acts that were left undone were of importance.

We may read about the "little way" and wonder whether or not the concept is strong enough to confront and challenge the bold-faced power supporting economic, social, and political systems and structures that create poverty and other injustices. Many religious social activists, from the past and in the present, would share similar doubts. Earlier in this chapter, we explored three different approaches to the connection between mysticism and social concern. Reinhold Niebuhr served as an example of a theologian who rejected mysticism because he thought it was too wrapped up in the eternal and avoided the concerns of the temporal world. Niebuhr also thought that without God's help human beings could accomplish little on their own to resolve social and economic problems. In *The Nature and Destiny of Man,* he argued that ". . . justice is an approximation to brotherhood (love) under conditions of sin."[22] The emphasis here is on creating structures oriented toward justice that in turn would create a stronger community and reflect God's love in the world.

However, Day is among those twentieth-century religious social activists who strongly emphasized personalism and believed that people needed to "start with themselves" if they wanted to address social problems and create systemic change. Howard Thurman and Martin Luther King Jr. were other well-known leaders who stressed personalism. Day's social mysticism was theologically grounded in her understanding of the incarnation and the mystical body of Christ and practically grounded in the contemplative tradition. "Room for Christ," an article Day published in December 1945, reflected on how God speaks in our time.

[N]ow it is with the voice of our contemporary that he speaks, with the eyes of store clerks, factory workers, and children that he gazes; with the hands of office workers, slum dwellers, and suburban housewives that he gives. It is with the feet of soldiers and tramps that he walks, and with the heart of anyone in need that he longs for shelter. And giving shelter or food to anyone who asks for it, or needs it, is giving it to Christ.[23]

God was revealed in the person and works of the historical Jesus and Christ was embodied in her own world by individuals practicing the works of mercy.

We might expect the word "justice" to be one of the terms most frequently appearing in the writings of someone whose daily activities were focused on charity *and* advocacy for people pushed to the margins of society. Very seldom did she use the word "justice" in her writing. Day more frequently chose to use the word love. We might consider reading through her work and replacing the word love with justice. Her use of the word "love" rather than "justice" is a reflection of her social mysticism. She frequently quoted John of the Cross, "Love is the measure by which we should be judged." In her essay "Love is the Measure" Day strongly connected loving others with doing justice:

> In the face of the approaching atom bomb test; . . .
> in the face of an approaching maritime strike; in the
> face of bread shortages and housing shortages; in the
> face of the passing of the draft extension, teenagers
> included, we face the situation that there is nothing
> we can do for people except to love them.[24]

For Day, love was a "divine weapon." The way in which Jesus laid down his life for others' sake, set aside his own self-interest, and loved both enemies and neighbors as friends was a symbol of the way in which we are all to love and bring about transformation.

CHAPTER FIVE

Living by an Ethic of Peace in a Culture Invested in War and Death

The term pacifism was first coined in Europe around the turn of the twentieth century to identify people who actively worked to limit and eliminate war. Today, casual conversations on the topic of pacifism are frequently informed by an understanding of peace as the absence of violent conflict. Popular definitions of peace from an Internet search include "freedom from disturbance," "quiet and tranquility," and "a state of security or order within a community established by law." In the United States, there is also a widespread assumption that peace can be established or won through violence and war. These assumptions would have informed popular discussions of peace and war in Dorothy Day's era as well. However, Day's understanding of pacifism was not based on these assumptions. For Day, pacifism meant much more than just the absence of violent conflict—pacifism was a distinctively Christian way of life.

Day's commitment to pacifism was firmly grounded in Jesus' teachings in the Gospels, sustained by daily spiritual disciplines, and practiced through her engagement in non-violent resistance movements. She looked to practices and traditions of the early church to define the fundamental means to commit to pacifism and resist what she sometimes called a "culture of death" by practicing voluntary poverty, engaging in manual labor, upholding "a sense of the primacy of the spiritual," and maintaining "a spirit of detachment from all things."

That is not to say that she isolated herself from social concern or protest movements. We have already discussed the three-pronged program of action that emerged from her conversations with Peter Maurin and in collaboration with many others. Day rejected the notion that responses and arguments rooted in materialistic assumptions could inspire a real vision for community. Catholic Workers argued for a "third alternative" known as distributism, an economic philosophy that seeks to subordinate economic life to the life of the whole community, including the spiritual life. Workers opposed state socialism and capitalism because they believed both emerged from materialist philosophy. One had to rely on personal responsibility to create change rather than the state. Moreover, capitalism, the free market economy, represented a vision and ordering of life for the whole creation that in her mind was diametrically opposed to Jesus' teachings. In theory, the success of the market in a capitalist society is determined by individual autonomy, but, in reality, people often have little individual autonomy in a system that values everything as a commodity with a price. Capitalism is fueled by competition between human beings, requires using the earth for human ends, and relies upon markets to determine the value of labor and the worth of goods. Common needs are all too often subordinated to the success of individuals or organizations created by them.

Divisions among people forged along lines of wealth, status, and social class were evident and obvious during Day's lifetime, but they were socially created. For Day, all people were equally valued by God and members of the body of Christ; that was the true and ultimate reality. She called on herself and other Workers to resist on every level a society, culture, and government predisposed toward creating wealth primarily for wealth's sake and well organized to bring death and devastation to those deemed enemies of the state. Spiritual disciplines steadied Day in the presence of the divine so that she could resist social, economic, and political systems and structures that place so many of the world's natural resources and people at the disposal and service of so few.

The next two chapters highlight significant events that formed and informed the way in which Day developed and lived by an ethic of peace. She was so actively involved in peacemaking efforts that her work for peace cannot possibly be discussed in a single chapter. Pacifism was her way of life—a daily challenge and daily practice. Day also traveled frequently, spoke to many groups, and cultivated a lay apostolate that would live by an ethic of peace within the hostile and violent social and political environs of the twentieth century. She nurtured the growth of hospitality houses forming around the country and spoke at colleges and universities as well as to members of union groups, religious orders, and activist organizations. This chapter explores the beginnings of and theological basis for Day's pacifism, connections Day made between the war machine and a capitalist economy, and the consistency of her pacifist stance, leading up to and through the horrific end of World War II.

Socialist and Christian Influences

Day first encountered pacifism in her work as a journalist covering peace news for a socialist newspaper, the *Call*. As early as 1917 she was assigned by an editor at the *Call* to cover anti-war activities during the weeks preceding the entrance of the United States into the First World War. President Woodrow Wilson was in the midst of his famous political flip-flop regarding the country's entry into the war. He won re-election on the basis that he had successfully kept the United States out of the war and then turned to advocate for the public to support entry into World War I. On April 2, 1917, Wilson delivered a now-famous speech to a joint session of Congress in which he identified German imperialism as a threat to "the free peoples of the world." Wilson called on Congress to act swiftly, and defined the object of declaring war in terms of vindicating "the principles of peace and justice in the life of the world as against selfish and autocratic power and to set up among the really free and self-governing peoples of the world . . . a concert of purpose and action,"[1] thereby making the world "safe for democracy." Day attended meetings and rallies for peace held at that time by groups such as the Emergency Peace Federation, the American Union Against Militarism, and the Collegiate Anti-Militarism League.

Socialists responded to World War I in a variety of ways. More moderate socialists, such as the French socialist Jean Jaurès, promoted social and economic reform as the means to establish peace. Radicals, like Vladimir Lenin, called for immediate reforms even if they had to be achieved through violent revolution. The *Call*, a paper tied to the Socialist Party of America, opposed the United States' entry into the war because of the injustices they identified in the social, economic, and political system: "[M]ilitarism, nationalism, and imperialism [were] dividing the laboring class and lining the pockets of the rich."[2]

Social class was not the only way that the First World War deeply divided people in the United States. The entrenched racism that gave rise to the Jim Crow laws, which were enacted in 1876, also informed the social, economic, and political system and structures. Many debates ensued about whether or not black people should have the "right" and "honor" to serve in the military or support the war effort. These debates unleashed a wave of racial violence across the country. Ida Wells-Barnett, a journalist who became well known for her honest reporting of the terrorism of lynch mobs, wrote articles and gave speeches in various forums about discrimination against black women who sought employment in factories that were supporting the war effort. Black soldiers were not allowed to serve alongside white soldiers in the United States military. Rather, they served with the French and took orders from French commanders. Returning to the United States after World War I and being forced to live under Jim Crow laws was an injustice too great for black veterans to bear. That experience of injustice helped to fertilize the soil from which the nonviolent movement for civil rights for African Americans would later grow.

Two of the most important issues raised by peace protestors were conscription and the Espionage Act of 1917. Many religious leaders had sympathies for socialist arguments concerning war even if they did not officially carry a "red card" or join the Socialist Party. Settlement worker

Jane Addams was among other Progressive reformers who adopted a pacifist stance. Addams helped to found the Women's International League for Peace and Freedom in 1915 and served as the organization's first president. In the years leading up to World War I, Protestant theologians such as Walter Rauschenbusch and Reinhold Niebuhr joined the ranks of protestors against the war. As the United States developed a taste for war, some of Rauschenbusch's colleagues in the Social Gospel came to believe that defeating Germany was essential to making progress toward the kingdom of God in America. Rauschenbusch cut against the

consensus building in support of the war among Protestants and spoke about Jesus' ideal of peace being a prescription for both personal ethics and national policy. Incidentally, Niebuhr, who later strongly criticized the Social Gospel, did not break away from pacifists until the 1930s.

Several organizations emerged during these years to galvanize efforts to prevent the United States from entering the war, including the Fellowship of Reconciliation (FOR) in the U.S. (1915), the American Friends Service Committee (1917), and the U.S. branch for the International League for Peace and Freedom (1919). Day, Rauschenbusch, and Niebuhr were all members of FOR, an ecumenical organization. Throughout the war years, the FOR in Europe and in the United States organized and supported organizations to defend civil liberties and the right for people to conscientiously object to war. Day remained a member after she converted to Catholicism. She was very active in the peace movement until she left the *Call* and her attentions were diverted to reporting for another socialist paper, the *Masses*.

Linking Pacifism Intentionally with Catholic Faith

After becoming Roman Catholic, Day more intentionally linked her pacifism to the practice of her faith. Ed Turner, a Worker who began as a volunteer in 1953, has been quoted saying: "Before Dorothy Day there was no Catholic pacifist theology."[3] The historical accuracy of Turner's claim could be tested and judged against prominent figures in the Catholic tradition like Francis of Assisi, but his comment remains instructive in defining the importance of Day's role in leading the peace movement among Catholics in the United States. From 1927 on, Day drew on her analysis of an unjust economic system, a literal reading of Jesus' teachings on peace in the Gospels, and the examples of figures in Christian history such as Francis of Assisi to provide the basis for her pacifism. Day rejected war and violence wholeheartedly and felt that there was no basis on which one could establish or discern rules for the just or appropriate use of violence. Her pacifism placed her at odds with the official position of the Catholic Church—a church known for establishing the tradition of "just war theory," a theory that makes room for justifiable cases of war and violence.

Christian peacemaking has ancient roots. Day grounded her pacifism in Jesus' teachings found in the Sermon on the Mount and the enumeration of what Catholics call the works of mercy. Jesus' Sermon on the Mount as it is recorded in Matthew links peace to economic conditions as the poor are blessed, the meek inherit the earth, and the hungry are filled. Faithful followers may even be persecuted for righteousness' sake. Peter Maurin thought that acts of war ran directly counter to acts of mercy. Jesus taught that you should feed the hungry, visit the sick, and care for those in prison, but nations in a state of war or conflict would intentionally create embargos, blockade other countries, and ensure that resources were limited so that people would starve—at which point people became desperate enough to surrender and so-called victory would be achieved. In this context, peace can be much more easily defined for the victor than the vanquished.

Christians have wrestled for centuries about the best way to embody an ethic of peace and to witness in every age to the distinctiveness of the community of faith in the midst of the world in which it exists. One of the perennial themes in discussions about the distinctiveness of the Christian community of faith is whether or not people of faith have the right to kill. Jesus taught that one should love one's neighbor as much as one's enemy. Even more so, Jesus taught that one should learn to love one's enemies as friends.

The identities of Christian communities in the first and second centuries were largely shaped by their status as minority groups. Stories about martyrs, confessors, and apostates were told about people who struggled to find the best ways to remain loyal to their beliefs and follow Christ in the midst of a sometimes hostile empire. Despite periods of persecution of Christians in the Roman Empire, the martyrs and confessors did not take up arms in response.

One of the most powerful stories is *The Martyrdom of Perpetua and Felicitas*, which dates from around 203 CE. The story is about Perpetua and Felicitas, two young women from North Africa. Perpetua is also the mother of a young child who, despite her father's pleading, refuses to renounce her faith. She is imprisoned with a slave named Felicitas, also the mother of an infant. As the story goes, both women are forced into the arena to fight with animals and gladiators. Milk drips from Felicitas' breasts as the women face their death. In the arena, Perpetua steadies and steers the sword being held in the hand of a novice gladiator into her own throat, but she herself does not take the sword in her own defense.

Day reflected on the importance of the story of Perpetua and other martyrs such as Polycarp, Ignatius of Antioch, and Blandina in her column in the *Catholic Worker*. Martyrs suffered with courage and identified with the "common lot of humanity" by not making their own survival a priority over the needs of others. She observed, "Why should I ask to be spared when I see the suffering of the family next door? Suffering borne with courage means to the devout mind a participating in the suffering of Christ and, if bravely endured, can lighten the sufferings of others. . . . It is an acceptance of the human condition."[4] The martyrs had the strength and courage to bear suffering and death rather than take up arms to ensure their own survival.

Questions about whether or not followers of Christ had the right to kill, particularly on behalf of an empire, gained an increased sense of importance after Emperor Constantine converted to Christianity in the fourth century and the Christian faith became the official religion of the Roman Empire. A generation after Constantine, the theologian Augustine contemplated how war could be justified to defend the rights of the weak and set the church on the course for developing the just war doctrine. Pacifists continue to see the just war doctrine as a way that Christianity began to accommodate itself to the surrounding culture.

In the Middle Ages, the medieval Catholic Church identified two different ethical levels within the church regarding witnessing for peace; the counsels of perfection and the precepts. According to Catholic doctrine, Christ gave certain rules for life that should be practiced by all followers. These rules, known as precepts, consisted primarily of the Ten Commandments as they were interpreted in light of gospel teachings. In addition to the precepts, Christ also taught principles, called the counsels of perfection, for people, such as those who lived in monastic communities, who desired to do more than the minimum. Francis of Assisi and his followers took vows to abide by these rules, which included poverty, chastity, and obedience. Legends about Francis of Assisi's rejection of war in the midst of the Crusades informed Day's position. She identified Francis as a "model for personalism, poverty, and pacifism." Day believed that Francis's compassion for people in poverty "laid the foundation of a new social order" and "struck a fatal blow to the feudal system."[5]

Later in Christian history, new church communities emerged as part of Protestant movements. Believers' churches or those considered by historians to be part of the Radical Reformation opposed a union between church and state and refused military service from their very beginnings. Mennonite, Brethren, and Quaker churches are known as the historic peace churches.

Day shared many commitments with members of the historic peace churches. She questioned loyalties given to what she called "Holy mother the state" and firmly grounded her own pacifism within the traditions of the early Christian communities of faith. Day thought that Catholic Workers, as members of a community based on the monastic model, should live by the counsels of perfection. It is surprising that she never voted even though she personally sought to resist on every level her own country's infatuation with competition, self-interest, and war. She was an anarchist in the sense that she did not think the state could be relied on as the primary instrument of change. For Day, the way to respond to the culture of death was to do what Maurin had envisioned: carve out space for "a new society to emerge within the shell of the old," to render as little to Caesar as possible, and to foster a society where it would be easier for people to be good.

Practicing Poverty

Voluntary poverty and pacifism were ways to resist or protest a culture invested in death. For Day and Catholic Workers, the practice of poverty was a "spiritual weapon" used to bring about peace. Catholic Worker Mary Durnin thought of "precarity" as one of the virtues of the Catholic Workers' life.[6] Poverty expressed one's sense of radical dependence on God and reflected a literal reading of Jesus' teachings in the Gospel of Matthew: " 'Therefore do not worry, saying, "What will we eat?" or "What will we drink?" or "What will we wear?" . . . But strive first for the kingdom of God and God's righteousness, and all these things will be given to you as well" (6:31, 33).

Thomas Merton, well-known Trappist monk, poet, spiritual social activist, and popular religious author, held great respect for Day and the Catholic Worker Movement. He described Dorothy Day's understanding of poverty in this way in a letter to the editor who had sent proofs of *Loaves and Fishes* to him for review: "Poverty for Dorothy Day is more than a sociological problem; it is also a religious mystery." Day herself characterized the paradoxical nature of poverty with these words: "I condemn poverty and I advocate it; poverty is simple and complex at once; it is a social phenomenon and a personal matter."[7] However, she did not falsely romanticize about poverty.

Day was well aware that when people in poverty asked for bread, they were too often handed stone. They were "betrayed by their teachers and their political leaders" and "robbed of their skills and made tenders of the machine."[8] She abhorred economic systems and structures that force people into poverty and denounced the practice of denying how one's own actions led to the impoverishment of others because both refuse to honor the full worth and dignity of human beings. Those living without access to basic necessities such as healthy food, clean water, sanitation, housing, education, and life-sustaining work experience chronic instability and often social exclusion.

At the same time, intentionally and voluntarily renouncing material wealth is liberating. Voluntary poverty or "holy poverty" turns one's attention away from accumulating material things and toward a focus on putting on Christ. Resources of both time and talent are freed to be shared with others. Day observed, "It is only if we love poverty that we are going to have the means to help others. If we love poverty we will be free to give up a job, to speak when we feel it would be wrong to be silent."[9] The practice of voluntarily renouncing one's worldly goods fosters an environment in which people can share and eliminates the social distance that material wealth creates between human beings.

Day was often called on to visit hospitality houses that emerged in locations across the country. Her understanding of the practice of poverty was informed by her awareness of class struggles, her interpretations of gospel teachings and the life and teachings of Francis of Assisi, and influenced by the liturgical movement. Voluntary poverty represented a form of radical egalitarianism as it accentuated Day's belief in the essential equality of all people because of the common fabric of their humanity and their creation in the image of God.

In contrast, the economic theory that informed a capitalist economy assumed that industry and market-driven society would fairly assess the value of people according to what they produced. Workers, however, were not valued for what they produced. Workers produced a great deal but did not get paid much when compared to upper management, who got paid a lot for not "producing" much at all. Women and people of color routinely were paid less even if they might be producing more. Worker pay was established according to the perceived market value of the particular task performed as opposed to the need to sustain an individual or family. Where, then, was equality in a capitalist economy?

Voluntarily choosing poverty was an act of solidarity, a form of peaceful, active, nonviolent resistance to the social and economic inequality, racism, sexism, and consumerism that characterized society in the United States during the early twentieth century. Practicing poverty also eliminated the distance created between people in society due to social class. In an article on "Poverty and Pacifism" Day said that voluntary poverty "means non-participation in those comforts and luxuries which have been manufactured by the exploitation of others . . . while our brothers [and sisters] suffer from lack of necessities, we will refuse to enjoy comforts."[10]

In houses of hospitality, voluntary poverty worked to equalize power. There was no power difference between the served and the servers. Dorothy had the view that the Catholic Worker Movement was not the same as philanthropy or "charity," which reifies social class distinctions. Catholic Workers sought to escape the condescending tone of "charity" by sinking into poverty themselves and continuing to give out of their own poverty. Recall that everyone was responsible for every task—from editing the paper to cleaning the toilets.

If money was needed for something, Workers were encouraged to pray for it. None of the Workers who would have been considered by outsiders as the "staff" of a house of hospitality took a salary for their work. Day never contributed to any kind of a retirement fund. She lectured and spoke all over the country and received royalties from sales of her books (often a paltry sum of 4 percent). Most of the money was given to the movement she founded, with the exception of some gifts to help her daughter, Tamar, and her family, who themselves lived in poverty. There were some practical concerns as well. Tom Cornell, one of the founders of the Catholic Peace Fellowship who also served as a staff person for that organization, remembered Day's shrewdness. If Day accepted large sums of money and deposited them in a bank account to serve as an "endowment" to secure continual support for the house of hospitality then there would be no reason for supporters to send their donations. Cornell said that's why Dorothy thought "you really need—a lot of people giving small sums of money. That way people feel an investment in the Worker. . . . It may be only a little bit, but it's real, and it means something to them."[11]

Resisting Economic Violence

The reexamination of money, jobs, and labor logically flowed for Day from one's commitment to voluntary poverty. Money should never be seen as a commodity to be traded but rather as a means of exchange. For Day, one should pray for the grace to give up jobs that do not serve the common good. She encouraged her readers to examine their consciences as to how their work provided for food, shelter, clothing, and care for a larger community. Examples she offered of work that did not advance the works of mercy included jobs in advertising, insurance, and banking. Recognizing how controversial Day's statement may seem in the contemporary context, it is important to more fully develop her argument concerning these forms of work.

Day believed that advertising unnecessarily elevated people's desires. At the turn of the twentieth century, retailing and advertising were innovations intended to increase the consumption of products that were mass-produced. The mass production of goods emphasized speedy and efficient production at the expense of worker well-being and placed in peril the rights of workers and their safety in the factories. Ads for products such as Coca-Cola emerged as early as the 1890s. Products became associated with well-being and even a sense of belonging to community as the advertising industry grew and marketing techniques developed. Ads were created to foster the belief that what fulfills one's needs and desires is having more access to goods and services, bigger and better homes, and finding security in the accumulation of wealth. She used the theological concept of "concupiscence" to describe the guilt of advertisers who were deliberately stimulating people's desires for things that they did not necessarily need or really want. Concupiscence is a theological concept identified with Augustine, who defined it as the sinful tendency to try to fulfill one's desires with material possessions. Day was among other religious social activists of her era who considered illusory the contemporary pursuit of that which was "more," "bigger," and "better." Accumulating worldly goods to satisfy one's needs and desires contributed to a social anxiety that made individuals focus more on the accumulation of things than the needs of the larger community. Day also argued that insurance companies and banks exploited people in poverty and others. "Banks and insurance companies have taken over land, built up farms, ranches, plantations, of 30,000, 100,000 acres, and have dispossessed the poor. Loan and finance companies have defrauded [those in poverty]."[12]

Rejecting the Notion that War Could be "Just"

Another form of violence, the violence of war, was such a familiar theme during Day's lifetime that she once observed that "[t]oday the whole world is in the midst of revolution." Some lists composed by historians of the major wars in the twentieth century cite over forty-five wars that involved nearly every region around the globe. Despite the widespread use of force as a means to settle conflicts, Day advocated nonviolent strategies as the only means for settling personal, national, or international disputes. Day critically assessed just war tradition and inspired many other

Christians across denominational lines to resist war. She urged Christians to adopt "a seeming impossibility—a training to the use of non-violent means of opposing injustice, servitude and a deprivation of the means of holding fast to the Faith."[13]

Earlier we encountered Augustine as the theologian and bishop responsible for the beginnings of just war theory. Another theologian, Thomas Aquinas, developed the principles of just war. The usage of the word "just" in the case of just war theory is something of a misnomer. The just war theory is not based on the idea that there is justice in war itself but rather establishes certain moral conditions that should be met before a nation declares war against another nation. The conditions that need to be met include, among other things, defending the rights of the weak, reasonable hope for success, consideration of the proportionality of force used, adequate discrimination of the impact of war on innocent civilians, and the understanding that war should only be used as a last resort.

The majority of Christian churches have adopted just war as their official position (Roman Catholic and Protestant mainline churches among them), excluding of course the historic peace churches (Mennonite, Church of the Brethren, and Quakers). Many churches in the United States still display both the Christian flag and the United States flag at the front of their sanctuaries. Christians in this sense have found ways to accommodate their beliefs to fit the needs of their nations.

Day maintained her pacifist position to resist death, destruction, violence, and war as a pattern and established norm for daily life. She read the biblical witness, particularly the Gospels, differently; one should "put away the sword" and "love your enemies" even when other countries rattled their sabers. She consistently emphasized in her writing the connection between war and the economy of the United States. During WWII, unemployment dropped because monies and labor were being invested in things such as patrolling and fortifying borders, the production of bombers, new technologies, military equipment, vehicles, and munitions, and in training soldiers to be effective killers. However, total indebtedness as a result of the war reached $200 billion or about 122 percent of the United States' gross domestic product. Such a tremendous investment in war set a pattern and course for the future of the nation's economy, which became dependent on the war "industry" to sustain its own growth.

Although she maintained fierce allegiance to the Roman Catholic Church, a just war church, she insisted that from its inception the *Catholic Worker* take a clear stance for total pacifism. Principles informing the Catholic Workers' pacifist position were clearly stated in an article on "Pacifism" published in the May 1936 edition of paper. Day wrote,

> We oppose class war and class hatred, even while we stand opposed to injustice and greed. Our fight is not "with flesh and blood but principalities and powers."
> We oppose also imperialist war.
> We oppose, moreover, preparedness for war, a preparedness which is going on now on an unprecedented scale and which will undoubtedly lead to war . . .
> Why not prepare for peace?[14]

Taking such a hard and clear stance would mean sacrificing some of the paper's popularity and alienating herself from the Catholic Workers who felt that they needed to join the war effort when the United States declared war on Germany and Japan.

Sustained by Spiritual Disciplines

Revisiting the concept of social mysticism is important in order to make the connection between liturgy and Day's work for social justice and peace. Inspired by the monastic model, life among Catholic Workers was shaped by work, worship, and prayer. The liturgical movement in the Roman Catholic Church, led by Father Virgil Michel, informed Day's and Maurin's practices and ideas as they were shaping and nurturing the Catholic Worker Movement. Day also found retreats an important resource for sustaining her energies. Sister Peter Claver, a sister of the Missionary Servants of the Blessed Trinity, was one of the first to recognize Day's need for a retreat and introduced her to Father Pacifique Roy some time in 1939. Dorothy had been on retreat before she met Fr. Roy but went to a convent that proved too austere. The bars on the cells of the nuns reminded Dorothy too much of her experience of prison.

In *The Long Loneliness,* Dorothy wrote that she was "spellbound" by Fr. Roy when she first heard his lectures on the Gospels. Fr. Roy found the Catholic Worker Movement intriguing and lectured on the theological basis the Gospels gave for their work. He believed that all Christians were called to live under vows of poverty, chastity, and obedience, not just those who committed themselves to officially sanctioned religious communities. Day began to make regular visits to see Fr. Roy in Baltimore and invited him to do a retreat for all the Catholic Workers.

During the war years, Father John Hugo of Pittsburgh led most of the retreats. Day also planned regular retreats for the Workers in the 1940s so that they would know what was expected of them.

Spiritual disciplines and retreats in the context of the Catholic Worker Movement should not be seen as a means of escape or just as a source of personal renewal. Retreats were a way of nurturing the spiritual life and cultivating deep inner resources. They gave Day a well from which she could draw spiritual strength and energy. From these spiritual disciplines she gained the courage to challenge society's worship of money, oppose the use of physical force as the means to make peace, join and support laborers standing on the picket lines, advocate for the right of individuals to conscientiously object to war, and remain steadfast in her pacifism even when other Catholic Workers disagreed with her.

An Unpopular Pacifist Stance in World War II

Day wrote a letter to all the Catholic Worker houses in the summer of 1940 that asked those who would not distribute the paper with its pacifist stance to disassociate themselves from the movement. She met quite a bit of resistance to her pacifist ideas, even among Catholic Workers. Some supported war efforts during World War II and did not see pacifism as an integral part of the movement as a whole. For many people, World War II was a clear example of a just war. The bombing of Pearl Harbor by the Japanese in December 1941, along with the effective media campaign initiated by the United States government, convinced a reluctant public of the inevitability and justice of war. Propaganda films such as the Frank Capra series *Why We Fight* provoked hatred for the Nazis and the German people and sometimes depicted Hitler with horns or fangs. The majority of the population came to disregard pacifism as a utopian fantasy that would leave too many innocent people defenseless.

From Day's perspective, pacifism was a form of active resistance, even in the case of World War II. Day was among a small minority of the United States population that adopted a pacifist stance. Those who objected to the war on religious grounds were primarily from the historic peace churches. There were a few examples of religious leaders from other traditions who, like Day, objected to the war. Social Gospeler Vida Dutton Scudder also advocated pacifism in WWII. Like Day, Scudder came to realize that the war had the effect of preserving the status quo and opposed war as a way of opting out of competitive society. Pacifists in WWII were harshly criticized, bore the brunt of name-calling such as "skunks" and "cowards," and were discriminated against in the marketplace. Even worse, pacifists faced the charge of anti-Semitism. Day replied to this charge in her column as she wrote:

> We do not take care of our own unemployed and hungry millions in city and country, let alone those beyond the seas. There is prejudice in our own country towards Jews, Negroes, Mexicans, Filipinos, and others, a sin crying to Heaven for punishment.[15]

In other words, Day saw no just cause for the moral ascendency of the United States as the legitimate basis for waging war.

The fact that Jewish people were being used as scapegoats by the Nazis was clear in Day's mind long before the United States entered the war. She submitted an article in November 1933 to Wilfrid Parsons, the editor of *America* magazine, which was intended to clarify the *Catholic Worker*'s position. However, Parsons declined to publish the article. Day wrote that Hitler and the Nazi party have "made the Jew as a race a scapegoat. They have fastened on it the ills of present-day society . . . [and] blamed the Jews for defeat during the war, for the inflation after the war, for the present ills of the capitalist system."[16] The article was intended to be a response to a problem that surfaced when the *Catholic Worker* paper was distributed at the end of several meetings held in Brooklyn where anti-Jewish speeches were made. Day disagreed with the distribution of the paper at these events and did not want the paper in any way to be associated with anti-Jewish sentiments.

Day actively confronted anti-Semitism by using nonviolent strategies. In 1935, she picketed *The Bremen*, a German ship sailing under the Nazi flag, as it arrived in New York's harbor. She helped to found the Committee of Catholics to Fight Anti-Semitism in 1939. As violence against Jews escalated in Europe, the *Catholic Worker* published an appeal for

United States citizens to open up their homes to Jewish people who needed asylum. Their plea largely went unheeded.

In July 1940, she traveled to Washington, DC, to offer her testimony along with other Catholic Workers, including Joe Zarrella, at the hearings before the Military Affairs Committee of Congress as they debated the passage of compulsory military training legislation. The *Catholic Worker* position was to oppose the instatement of a draft on the basis that conscription was founded on "pagan precedent" and "abhorrent to the spirit of Christianity." The bill was revised after the hearings and included provisions for conscientious objection to war.

The letter Day sent to Catholic Workers in August 1940 not only clarified her position on pacifism but also included a handbook on conscientious objection. In the letter she mentioned that there were Catholic Worker groups who disagreed with the stance of total pacifism. She argued that Catholic Workers were trying to live by the counsels of perfection and asked those who were unable to take a pacifist stance in war not to say that they represented the *Catholic Worker* position.

Day clearly identified the evil and racism of Nazi ideology, but she also saw other injustices created by war. In one of the articles she wrote for the July-August 1940 edition of the paper, "And There Remained Only the Very Poor," Day likened the experience of people in poverty being left behind when Paris was evacuated in June 1940 to that of impoverished people trapped in New York City during a summer heat wave. "The poor cannot get away," she observed.

When the United States declared war on Japan, Germany, and their allies, the *Catholic Worker* headline read: "Our Country Passes From Undeclared War to Declared War We Continue our Pacifist Stand." Day clearly named the Catholic Workers' pacifist "manifesto":

> We are still pacifists. Our manifesto is the Sermon on
> the Mount, which means that we will try to be
> peacemakers. Speaking for many of our conscientious
> objectors, we will not participate in armed warfare or
> in making munitions, or by buying government
> bonds to prosecute the war, or in urging others to
> these efforts.[17]

In other articles, she emphasized the refusal of the Desert
Fathers to be part of war efforts. She urged young men not
to register for the draft and declared that if women were
forced to register she would not comply. Her characteriza-
tions of the war as "evil," "incompatible with a religion of
love," and the draft as a form of state "enslavement" must
have been seen as incendiary. Her steadfast pacifist position
impacted the paper. The readership and circulation of the
paper greatly diminished as a result of its pacifist stance.
Some Catholic Workers remained resolute in their pacifism,
but many left the movement and enlisted their services in
the war effort. The war industry also provided jobs for the
masses of people who had been out of work. Unemployment dropped and the increase of employment resulted in
fewer numbers of people standing in soup lines or in need
of places to stay. These changes meant the closure of fifteen
houses of hospitality.

There were not many Catholics who staunchly opposed
World War II. Archbishop Francis Joseph Spellman, bishop
of the diocese of New York and vicar apostolic for the
United States Armed Forces during the Second World War,
mobilized Catholics to support the war. The scope of his
political and ecclesiastical influence enabled him to acquire
the nickname "the Powerhouse." He consulted with many
political leaders and was chosen by President Roosevelt to
pay official visits to Europe, Africa, and the Middle East
during the war. Spellman opposed the *Catholic Worker*'s

pacifist stance during the years leading up to WWII. In 1946, Pope Pius XII elevated Spellman to the College of Cardinals because of his influence and national prominence. As you can imagine, Spellman was always anxious about Day being regarded as a voice of the Catholic conscience in the United States. Day and Spellman would butt heads several times during his tenure as bishop of New York between the years of 1939–1967.

In September 1943, Day announced in the paper her plan to take a year away from the New York house of hospitality and the *Catholic Worker*. She decided to take a sabbatical while on a retreat led by Father John Hugo. Fr. Hugo's retreats focused on cultivating silence and clarifying how one's actions reflected the divine. This particular retreat in the summer of 1943 emphasized the significance of baptism as planting a seed of holiness and was intended to inspire retreatants to do everything for the love of God. Afterward, Dorothy appeared to feel the need to reflect on her own life and work.

In their book *The Catholic Worker Movement: Intellectual and Spiritual Origins*, Mark and Louise Zwick describe Day's sabbatical as a "desert" experience in which she tried to cultivate practices of silence, solitude, and prayer. The first month of her sabbatical was spent in Libertyville, Illinois at a training center for women of the lay apostolate. She later moved to St. Bernadette, a Dominican convent in Farmingdale, Long Island, where she could be closer to her daughter, Tamar. Tamar, who was seventeen at that time, had enrolled in an agricultural school there. Dorothy made only two entries in her diary between September 1943 and February 1944. When she began journaling again she wrote about time spent to examine her conscience and practice, reflected on the "sins" of her past, and considered the difficulties she personally faced as she tried to cultivate silence.

Ultimately, she concluded that a life of silence and solitude was not for her. Day's returned to the paper and her life on Mott Street after a six-month sabbatical.

Innocence Lost

At the end of World War II, the world witnessed the effects of death and devastation in a way that it had never seen before. Historians estimate that about 60 million people died across three continents. Approximately 40 million of those who died were civilians. Cityscapes and people's lives lay in ruins all across Europe. The war in Japan met an even more visibly horrific end as the United States forces used the first atom bombs in warfare. The military necessity of dropping the atom bombs to end the war was heavily debated at that time. What was not debatable was the moral responsibility and loss of a sense of innocence for the United States. An estimated 135,000 people died as the result of the bomb called "Little Boy" that was dropped on Hiroshima, Japan on August 6, 1945. Three days later another bomb nicknamed "Fat Man" was dropped on Nagasaki. About 50,000 people died as the result of the second bomb. Five out of six of the people who died in these Japanese cities were civilians. The United States could not wash its hands of the blood shed in this tragedy.

Day's pen recorded the *Catholic Worker* response to Hiroshima in the September 1945 issue of the paper,

> President Truman. True man; what a strange name, come to think of it. We refer to Jesus Christ as true God and true Man. Truman is a true man of his time in that he was jubilant. He was not a son of God, brother of Christ, brother of the Japanese, jubilating as he did. He went from table to table on the cruiser

which was bringing him home from the Big Three conference, telling the great news; 'jubilant' the newspapers said. Jubilate Deo. We have killed 318,000 Japanese.[18]

At the end of the article she observed that God is still creator of all and that Jesus had already passed judgment on nuclear war. She paraphrased two passages from the Gospels to emphasize her point. " 'You know not of what spirit you are. The Son of Man came not to destroy souls but to save.' " He said also, 'What you do unto the least of these my brethren, you do unto me.' "[19] We will turn our attention to the expanding scope of Day's peacemaking efforts in the next chapter.

CHAPTER SIX

Spreading a Gospel of Peace in the Age of Nuclear War

After the end of World War II, people around the globe were forced to confront the cruelty and horror of the Holocaust, a reality that most would rather have continued to deny. Terrifying stories were told by the survivors of death camps and the soldiers who liberated them. News media reported the progress of trials of war criminals. The news drew attention to hungry people living in cities being reconstructed across Europe and Asia, wounded soldiers returning from their tours of duty, and the impact of the atomic bombs dropped on Japan. While many religious leaders and theologians pondered God's goodness in the face of such destruction, there was at the same time a spirit and sense of righteousness that pervaded Allied countries after their victory over Europe and Japan. The victory seemed clean; good triumphed over evil, and peace had been restored. It seems logical that people longed to return to some sense of normalcy after the war's end. However, Day believed that the kind of living most people in the United States assumed to be normal was the root cause of war. Going back just to live as one pleases was something she saw as a terrible mistake.

Day and the Catholic Worker Movement as a whole continued to try to live in the "little way" after WWII and gave more attention to anti-war demonstrations. These demonstrations reflected Day's broader pacifist commitments and ever-increasing consciousness of the systemic connections between the economic systems and structures capable of creating massive wealth for the few while at the same time submerging others into poverty. Neither the social disease of racism nor the world's history of colonialism could be ignored when examining inequalities in wealth and access to power. Violence and war were being used as the means to protect the interests of individual nations at the expense of people living in poverty and to maintain the power and privilege of Western democracies.

Day had built a strong network of support by the mid-1940s that enabled her to expand her witness for peace. The groundwork for the Catholic Worker Movement had already been laid. People's attention in the U.S. became more focused on the global community for some very obvious reasons. The *Catholic Worker* received letters from people, particularly Catholics, who lived in Europe and Asia. Appeals were made in the paper for clothing and food to be sent to the hungry. Day urged her readers to send what they could.

The Cold War was on the horizon even before the end of WWII. Political leaders stoked the fear of communism in the United States and among the Allies. Day confronted the red-baiting and fear mongering that dominated so much of public debate during the Cold War with a gospel of peace. When the United States waged war in Korea and Vietnam, she spoke out against the use of war as an instrument to protect the interests of the wealthy. In response to the ugly racism and hate speech that polluted culture and society in the United States, Day spoke about love and inclusion within the mystical body of Christ.

Dorothy had always traveled, but she was invited to speak to many more groups in the United States and beyond the nation's borders—churches, newly formed hospitality houses, unions, religious orders, colleges and universities, and activist organizations. She engaged in a variety of peace missions including traveling to Cuba, showing her solidarity with the movement for civil rights for African American people, advocating for rights for migrant farm workers, and praying for peace in Rome as her own church considered its role in the modern world. New workers and friends allied themselves with the movement, including Ammon Hennacy, Thomas Merton, Tom Cornell, and Philip and Daniel Berrigan. Their leadership also added to the movement's vibrancy and creative imagination for advocacy. Day and many other Catholic Workers birthed, shaped, led, and supported what would later be recognized as some of the most significant movements and organizations for peace, civil rights, and social change in the twentieth century.

It is not possible to chronicle all of Day's peacemaking activities from the 1950s onward because pacifism was simply her way of life. Collectively, the snapshots offered in this chapter will illustrate the breadth and scope of Day's pacifism between 1950 and until her death in 1980. Day gained a clear, mature, and profound understanding of the systemic and structural connections between poverty, racism, and violence. Her influence and peacemaking activities extended far beyond the walls of the hospitality house and the fields of Tivoli.

"Why not prepare for peace?"

United States residents first witnessed on their own soil the destruction that an atom bomb was capable of causing when a bomb named "Trinity" was tested in Los Alamos, New Mexico, on July 16, 1945. Photographs taken of bomb tests and the ominous mushroom clouds containing toxic radioactive particles unfurling into the sky are recognizable symbols of nuclear weapons even decades later. For Christians, particularly those who find themselves firmly rooted in Catholic traditions, naming the bomb "Trinity" could not have been more ironic or misguided. For Catholics, the concept of the "Trinity" is not only a description of God's nature but also a symbol of and model for human relationships defined in terms of sharing, reciprocity, cooperation, and love. Day raised this question in response to the testing of the bomb in the editorial she wrote in the *Catholic Worker*: "Who would deliver me from this body of death? We can only suggest one thing—destroy the two billion dollars' worth of equipment that was built up to make the atomic bomb; destroy all the formulas, put on sack cloth and ashes, weep and repent."[1]

Red-baiting, instilling fear, and preparing for more war were the most familiar responses for political leaders as well as the majority of the public even after witnessing the death and destruction caused by WWII. Tensions between countries influenced by Western concepts of democracy and Communist countries were already evident during WWII and continued to escalate after the war ended. Russia, like so many other countries, suffered tremendous losses during the war. Twenty million Russians died. Soviet Premier

Joseph Stalin called for a buffer zone to be created between Western Europe and Russia. The leaders of Allied armies, Winston Churchill among them, signed what was known as the "percentages agreement" that allowed Stalin to take control of countries where the Russian Army was the lead in defeating the Nazis. Early in 1946, Churchill visited the United States and called for a post-war alliance against Communist Russia in a speech where he used his famous term "the iron curtain."

The United States began aid through the Marshall Plan in 1948 as part of a larger effort to reconstruct European economies after the war and to aid and strengthen non-Communist Europe. An editorial was published in the *Catholic Worker* in December of 1947 as the Marshall Plan was being developed. Workers opposed the plan because it abrogated their sense of Christian personal responsibility and extended an economic system they believed to be "unjust and immoral."[2] They thought that it was another example of modern industrial capitalism taking advantage of people's destitution and forcing all Europeans to conform to capitalist ideology. Instead, they called for people to live by Jesus' revolutionary principles to love one's neighbor as oneself.

By 1949, all the governments of Eastern Europe, with the exception of Yugoslavia, fell under the political leadership of Stalinist regimes. The North Atlantic Treaty Organization (NATO) formed a political and military alliance in April of that same year. Twelve countries were founding members of NATO: Belgium, Canada, Denmark, France, Iceland, Italy, Luxembourg, the Netherlands, Norway, Portugal, the United Kingdom, and the United States. By August 1949, the Soviets themselves had successfully tested an atomic bomb. The Cold War was on.

You will remember that Day was sympathetic with socialist causes. She worked as a journalist for socialist newspapers

125

during the first Red Scare (1919–1921) and maintained several strong alliances, particularly through her friends, family, and with those whom she worked as a journalist. She was connected to Rayna Simons Prohme, Mike Gold, and Elizabeth Gurley Flynn, who all became members of the Communist Party. Day's friends in her early life were revolutionaries even though she herself never joined the Communist Party. However, she did not think that Christianity stood in opposition to communism any more than other political parties.

Many of the countries in Central and Eastern Europe also had large Roman Catholic and Greek and Russian Orthodox populations. Those who identified themselves primarily by their religious identities were disenfranchised and discounted when agreements were signed between political leaders. Day appeared to hold some special concern for the people of Hungary who were mentioned on a regular basis in her column and had been harshly repressed by the Communist regime. There were and continue to be large populations of Catholic, Orthodox, and Reformed Christians in Hungary. Cardinal József Mindszenty, the archbishop of Esztergom and highest Catholic official in Hungary during the 1940s and early 1950s, became for Roman Catholics and many other Christians living on the other side of the iron curtain the symbol of religious oppression and depth of the political reach of the Communists. Mindszenty spoke out against the oppression of the Jews by the fascists during WWII and then again voiced his dissent against the lack of political freedom afforded under the Communist regime. He was arrested in 1948 on charges of treason, a charge that resulted in his sentencing to life in prison. When a reformist government took power for a brief period of time in 1956, Mindszenty was able to find refuge at the American Embassy in Budapest and secure safe passage to Austria.

Day spoke out strongly against the repression of church officials by Communist leaders, but she was also equally disillusioned by the United States governments' repression of Communists. Their political strategies bore too many similarities. She made her position clear in her essay "Our Brothers, The Communists":

> Certainly we disagree with the Communist Party, but so do we disagree with the other political parties, dedicated to maintaining the status quo. We don't think the present system is worth maintaining. We and the Communists have the common idea that something else is necessary, some other vision of society must be held up and worked toward.[3]

Surely her statement cut against the grain of powerful politicians such as Senator Joseph McCarthy and the unpopular sentiment toward communism.

Day also stood in opposition to the anticommunist position held by some vocal Catholic bishops, particularly Archbishop Fulton Sheen and Cardinal Francis Spellman. Sheen was widely known for his televised speeches and sermons that condemned "the evils of Communism." As you will recall, Spellman was celebrated by the Roman Catholic Church during his lifetime for supporting war efforts beginning with World War II. He was also adamantly against liberalism in both church and politics. Day stood diametrically in opposition to the "Powerhouse," Cardinal Spellman, in 1949. She was one of the few who took the risk to publicly support the United Cemetery Workers. Spellman was against a strike held by the union at the largest Catholic cemetery in New York City. He accused the gravediggers of being influenced by Communism, an inflammatory charge to make during the Cold War and especially in New York at that time. There was a trial going on at the federal courthouse of twelve men who had been charged as Communist conspirators. It appeared that the Cardinal intended to cast the strike in the shadow of that trial.[4]

The United Cemetery Workers were shocked by the Cardinal's accusation. They had made a collective bargaining agreement with the diocese, their employer, for the previous two years. Their work week was defined as a six-day, forty-eight hour work week for which they were paid about $60.00 a week, and they were asking for the same rate of pay for a five-day, forty-hour work week and overtime for working more than eight hours a day or on Saturday. The diocese refused the agreement and offered only a cost-of-living increase recommended by the Bureau of Labor Statistics, a bit less than 3 percent.

The gravediggers union began striking in late January of 1949. With limited outside support, they quickly ate up their own small savings, receiving only a small amount of financial assistance, $5,000, from the transport workers. Catholic Workers and the Catholic Association of Trade Unions were strongly in favor of their action. Things became more heated as the strike continued over the next two months. The Cardinal tried to meet with the union workers in February, but the meeting did not come to a satisfactory conclusion for the union. By the beginning of March, more than a thousand bodies lay unburied at the cemetery and sixty bodies were arriving daily. Cardinal Spellman broke the strike on March 2, 1949, Ash Wednesday on the liturgical calendar, as he announced that he and local seminarians would cross the picket line and dig the graves.[5] Day was incensed.

She happened to be in Louisville, Kentucky, when she heard of the Cardinal's announcement. She was speaking to the students of Ursuline College and Loretto High School on "Love and Hate in the Modern World."[6] Jack Ford, who was a professor at the Ursuline school at that time and later taught at Bellarmine College, recalled Day's reaction to the news. He was having lunch with Day in the cafeteria at Ursuline College. When she heard about Spellman breaking the strike, she bristled and immediately got up from the table to go make a phone to call the Cardinal. Day followed up that call with a letter written on March 4, 1949, the same day she spoke to the students at Ursuline College. Her letter explained her understanding of the teachings of the church, especially *Rerum Novarum,* underscored the dignity of all workers, emphasized peace, and highlighted her labor theory. She pleaded with the Cardinal to meet with the union to settle on a mutually beneficial agreement, but to no avail. Spellman also refused to invite a mediator to facilitate negotiations. The strike ended on March 11, 1949, when the trustees of St. Patrick's Cathedral offered an 8 percent increase in pay for the gravediggers with the same forty-eight hour, six-day work week, and the gravediggers returned to work.

Progressive Catholic papers and magazines did not let the dust settle after the strike and remained strongly critical of the Cardinal's actions. The *Catholic Worker* ran an article in April 1949 about Spellman's responses to the strikers under the title "Cardinal Brings to End New York Strike." In the article, Day accused the Cardinal of giving weak advice to Catholic laypeople and trustees of St. Patrick's Cathedral. Both the Cardinal and the lay trustees failed to "treat Catholic working men as human beings and brothers."[7]

This would not be the last time Day confronted Cardinal Spellman. Two years after the strike, on March 3, 1951, Day was summoned by Monsignor Edward Gaffney to the Archdiocesan Chancery office. Gaffney told Day that the paper should cease using the term "Catholic" in its title because the Workers' positions were not always consistent

with official church teachings. Day knew that Gaffney's request also reflected the Cardinal's opinion.

Worker Resistance to Anti-Communism and Air Raid Drills

The unfair treatment of and attitudes toward Communists by both political and church leaders in the United States greatly disturbed Day. So many public resources were directed toward fighting Communism that the systemic causes of violence, economic injustice, and war were not being given adequate attention. A committee was created in 1938 by the House of Representatives that was called the House Un-American Activities Committee (HUAC) reflected the

general atmosphere of hysteria created by government officials during the Cold War. HUAC maintained the goal of
investigating disloyalty among citizens and kept files on
many people suspected of communist sympathies between
the years 1947 and 1975. Some of the suspects included
religious leaders such as Social Gospeler Vida Dutton Scudder, Day, and many other Catholic Workers. President Tru-
man required a loyalty oath of all federal employees in
1947. The McCarran Act, an anticommunist law, was also
passed around this time in 1950.

Day thought that hatred of Communism spurned more
violence and death. Her steadfast pacifism and sympathy
toward socialist ideals throughout the Cold War created
controversy particularly within the Catholic Church. On the
one hand, she was able to garner the support of many
Catholics and was often asked to speak in churches, paro-
chial schools, colleges, and universities around the country.
On the other hand, most Catholics held views more similar
to those advocated by Archbishop Sheen and Cardinal
Spellman. Her return to Louisville in 1952 to speak at both
Ursuline College and newly founded Bellarmine College
illustrates the kind of controversy stoked by her views and
disagreements with the Catholic community over pacifism
and socialism.[8]

Day was invited to speak to Professor Jack Ford's philosophy class at Bellarmine. In 1952, Bellarmine was an
all-male school and the United States was engaged in the
Korean War. Father John Loftus, the dean of the college
and a former military chaplain, reacted against a pacifist
being invited to speak to a class of draft-age men. Loftus
confronted Ford for inviting Day to speak in his class:
"You've disturbed my students!" Ford, a very good philosophy professor who wanted to expand the minds and consciences of his class, responded: "That is exactly what I

intended to do." He heard nothing more from the dean about Day's lecture and felt no repercussions for extending an invitation to her to speak in his class.

The discontent expressed by Loftus reflects not only the struggle of a dean at a newly founded institution, but also the way in which Day's pacifist commitments and socialist sympathies spoke directly into a broader cultural ferment. Anticommunist attitudes were so prominent in the Catholic Church and society throughout the Cold War. Loftus later distinguished himself as an "activist-educator." Among other things, he was involved in the anti-war movement in the 1960s, organized in 1964 (before the conclusion of the Second Vatican Council) what was believed to be the first regular service in which Protestant and Catholics worshiped together in Louisville, and took part in the 1965 civil rights march from Selma to Montgomery.[9] It is worth speculating whether or not Day's speech at Bellarmine contributed to Loftus's later activism. One can't be sure, but I think it is very likely as the authenticity and integrity of her pacifism inspired many people who heard her speak.

A highly publicized court case in the early 1950s concerning the suspected criminal actions of a couple named Julius and Ethel Rosenberg provides another illustration of the strong resistance to communism in the United States. Julius and Ethel were both children of Russian immigrants. The Rosenbergs were accused and convicted of espionage with no recommendation from the jury for mercy. They proclaimed their innocence. Day felt great empathy for the couple. She was with her grandchildren when Julius and Ethel Rosenberg were executed in Sing Sing prison in Ossining, New York, and the event distracted her attention away from her family.

In the 1950s, the federal government went so far as to begin to prepare United States citizens for the possibility of nuclear war and urged them to make preparations for their own survival. Strategies used to prepare citizens for Communist attack on United States soil were referred to by the government as "Civil Defense." The movie *Duck and Cover* was a film geared toward children that taught them to seek shelter if the United States were under attack just like Bert the turtle seeks shelter by hiding in his shell. Of course, children, unlike turtles, don't carry shelters on their backs so they had to learn to find their own. A whole industry sprang up that sold affordable shelters for those seeking protection from nuclear fallout. In 1955, the state of New York announced the passage of a law that required all citizens to participate in statewide civil defense drills. Anyone who did not comply with the new law would be subject to a fine of $500 and to arrest. Peace activists at the time observed that the new law was based on two faulty assumptions: the law assumed the inevitability of war and that many people could actually survive a nuclear explosion. Resistance to "Civil Defense" and air raid drills mounted quickly among advocates for peace. The Fellowship of Reconciliation launched a campaign called "Shelters for the Shelterless." Some houses of hospitality placed on display signs reading, "This House Has No Fallout Shelter, Peace is Our Only Protection."

Day thought the drills promoted the illusion that nuclear war was survivable and therefore not an option to be completely rejected. Moreover, she believed that her refusal to participate in the drills was an act of penance. As the citizen of the country that had been first to develop the hydrogen bomb and first to drop the atom bomb on citizens of another country, she felt the need to highlight her nation's sins. Who in Hiroshima or Nagasaki had access to information or shelter that would have protected them from the bombs dropped on their cities? Day and other Catholic

Workers decided to protest by refusing to seek shelter during New York City's air raid drills. The first air raid drill occurred on June 15, 1955. During the drill, Dorothy gathered with twenty-eight other people, including activist Ammon Hennacy, to stage a protest in the park in front of city hall in Lower Manhattan.

Air raid drills occurred once a year from 1955 until 1961. Each year the Catholic Workers staged a protest. The protestors were arrested for disobeying the law for each demonstration that occurred between 1955 and 1959. In 1955, Day and Hennacy pleaded guilty, stating in court their "loyalty to God even at the risk of disobedience and subversion to the coercive State."[10] The harshest sentence that Dorothy received was thirty days in jail for her participation in the protest of 1957. In 1958, when she, Ammon, and others stayed above ground, they received a suspended sentence. Public sentiment had changed by the 1960s. Other groups such as SANE (the Committee for Sane Nuclear Policy) joined the Workers in protest when they gathered in the park in 1961. That year, nearly 2,000 people came.

Visiting Allies at Koinonia Farms

The movement for civil rights for African Americans began to reach its peak during the same time that the public's attention was being directed toward communism and the Cold War. Rights for African American people had always been on the *Catholic Worker*'s agenda. The connection between racism and the plight of workers was present early on in the paper. James Forbes, senior minister emeritus of Riverside Church in New York City, has made the observation that when civil rights leaders and other activists began to see clearly just how much United States culture and society were immersed in toxic waters of race hatred, colonialism, and systemic violence, they became too dangerous and threatening to the current social order to be tolerated. Remember that Martin Luther King Jr. himself was assassinated in Memphis, Tennessee, when he was called there to show his solidarity with striking black garbage workers, the lowest-paid laborers.

In April 1957, Day traveled to Koinonia Farm at Americus, Georgia, in an intentional effort to show her solidarity with the "fear and suffering" felt by the community there that was being intimidated, shot at, and boycotted by white supremacists. Clarence and Florence Jordan founded Koinonia Farm in 1942 as a model for racial reconciliation that was theologically informed by their understanding of the incarnation and based on Jesus' principles of nonviolence and sharing. The community was not intended to be utopian, but it was based on shared ownership of property and mission. Clarence introduced both theological novelty and agricultural innovation at the farm. He developed a mobile peanut harvester that could be used by other farmers. A "cow library" was established at Koinonia where others could check out cows in order to have milk. He also built what came to be known as luxurious chicken coops that enabled hens to produce eggs in abundance. Koinonia became a model fledgling farm. Early on, they hired a black sharecropper to join in their labor. Whites and blacks worked together and sat together at the same table to share meals. These practices soon became the target of the hostility of the local Ku Klux Klan.

Another national event increased the attention given to Koinonia Farm by white supremacists. In 1954, the Supreme Court decided to desegregate schools. Clarence helped two black students with their applications to a formerly all-white college in Atlanta. Violence against and hostility toward Koinonia escalated. Pastor and social activist Joyce Hollyday shared an interview that she held with Florence Jordan about her experience of the violence in an article published in *Sojourners* in 1979. White supremacists harassed the farm by peppering the buildings with gunshots, burning buildings, cutting down fences, stealing crops, dumping garbage on the property, ruining a truck engine by putting sugar in the gas tank, chopping down a large grove of fruit trees, and holding their own economic embargo against products sold by the farm.[11]

Day heard the story of Koinonia, which had gained some national attention, and decided to take a thirty-six hour bus ride to Georgia. Clarence, who was accompanied by his son Lennie, met Dorothy at the bus station. She went there for an extended stay during the last two weeks of Lent and Holy Week, and planned to work on the farm. Her record

of the visit appeared in the form of several letters that she wrote for her column for the May 1957 issue of the *Catholic Worker* paper. The letters reference Day meeting representatives from the National Council of Churches and the Southern Baptist Convention and hearing Jordan talk about his own travels. She also told stories about her experience of working in the farm's kitchen, traveling with Florence and Lennie to buy seed peanuts in Albany and being called "dirty Communists and nigger lovers," and then taking a shift on the farm's night watch. She took a turn sitting up with another member of the community named Elizabeth to keep watch for people trying to start fires. Their shift was from 12:00 to 3:00 am. She wrote in her letter, "[A]t one thirty, we [were] sitting in a station wagon, under a flood light, under a huge oak tree, and a car slowed up, as it passed and peppered the car with shot. We heard sounds of repeated shots—a regular gunfire, and we were too startled to duck our heads."[12] Day felt "shaken" and commented that she had never been shot at before.

The description of Jordan that Day included in the letters she wrote from Koinonia Farm to the *Catholic Worker* during her visit and that was later included in her column "On Pilgrimage" reveal her strong feelings of being allied with the members of the Koinonia community in a common mission. She wrote,

> The entire way of life of the community—the firm foundation of non-ownership is a challenge to the capitalist system of America. If others followed the example . . . to build up a new society within the shell of the old by the hard labor of their hands, an oasis where there would be common ownership, and the responsibilities which went with that common ownership, the problems of tenant farming, share

cropping, day laborers, peonage, distribution, debt, and so on, would be solved, for Negro, for white, for Mexican, for Puerto Rican, for all.[13]

Throughout the 1960s, Day showed her solidarity with the movement for civil rights through contributions, money, prayers, and by working within their own local community.[14]

Investigating Cuba

Revolutions were occurring all around the world in the mid-1950s in response to political repression, a long history of colonialism, poverty, and the unequal distribution of wealth—examples include Puerto Rico, Indonesia, and Cuba. The Cuban revolution became of particular concern to United States political leaders, as Cuba is such a close neighbor, only about ninety miles off the coast of Florida.

Cuba holds a wealth of natural resources and fertile soil for farming. The country was colonized in the sixteenth century by the Spanish, who exploited the indigenous people and imported slaves to farm the land. Slavery was not abolished in Cuba until the late nineteenth century. The United States maintained close ties with Cuba during the first half of the twentieth century, partly due to the American sweet tooth. Trade agreements between the two countries ensured preferential treatment for sugar.

> [U]nder the Sugar Act of 1956, the United States formally secured a Cuban commitment to purchase rice in exchange for continued preferential treatment of sugar. Cuba purchased about 75 percent of all US rice exports. Between 1955 and 1959, domestic production grew about 10 percent and rice imports more than 40 percent.[15]

This type of trade agreement essentially prevented Cuba from diversifying its own economy. Historian Marifeli Pérez-Stable observes that between 1952 and 1958 national wages barely grew, but most important, in areas where the economy was dominated by sugar production the wages actually declined. The vast majority of the Cuban people remained incredibly poor. About one third of the labor force did not have access to full-time employment. Cuba's literacy rates were relatively high for the time; the fourth highest in Latin America in the 1950s. Educational attainment, however, was not as strong. Most in Havana had some level of primary education. In 1953, only 6.9 percent of the population of Havana graduated from high school or vocational school; 2.2 percent of the people living in rural surrounding areas attained a similar level of education.[16]

It was out of this context that Fidel Castro emerged as a leader of a violent revolt. Castro was the son of a wealthy farmer who acquired leftist political tendencies while studying at the University of Havana. He was also a lawyer and a Roman Catholic who became a violent revolutionary. He used guerrilla tactics to fight and eventually overthrow the rule and armed forces of Fulgencio Batista y Zaldívar. Batista was a United States-backed military leader during WWII who later became a dictator within Cuba. Castro's efforts, along with other guerrilla warfare used across the country, ultimately forced Batista to resign and flee. Castro became the prime minister of Cuba in February 1959 and had about 550 of Batista's associates executed. Soon after he came to power Castro suspended elections and named himself "President for Life." After gaining power, tensions escalated when United States leaders who distrusted Castro backed and set up training camps for Cuban exiles to invade their homeland. The Bay of Pigs invasion was launched and failed in April 1961. Castro saw a greater need for allies, and he strengthened ties between Cuba and the Soviet Union.

The *Catholic Worker* featured a series of articles in 1959 about the Cuban revolution. Many of them characterized the revolution as "highly desirable." In its early years, the American left favorably viewed the Cuban revolution. The articles in the *Catholic Worker* elicited a strong response among the paper's readers. Several readers wrote letters to the editor to ask Day to clarify the paper's stance on the Cuban Revolution. Day responded to readers' request in the July-August issue: "This is extremely difficult for us to do, since we are religious in our attitude . . . and we are also revolutionaries, in our own fashion."[17] Her article included a reference to a visit that she had paid to a poor community in New York that was being served by a religious order. The religious order, with the support of the larger church, had spent $85,000 building a residence for the nuns to serve the people. However, Day had personally visited Puerto Rican families as large as twelve who were living in two-room apartments in New York. This story highlighted the irony of the church serving the poor in comfort. The difficulty of the situation in Cuba and with Castro was that his interest was being on the "side of the poor." Day found herself with some conflicted loyalties.

Day decided to travel to Cuba in September 1962 to clarify her position for readers. She departed the United States with the goal of seeing "for herself life under Castro's communism, especially farming communes, the life of the family, and religious freedom."[18] By that time, the United States government had placed an embargo on Cuba that included severe restrictions on travel and commerce between the two countries. Day was unable to fly to Cuba so she had to travel by boat. She wrote a series of articles for the *Catholic Worker* which focused on the country's wealth of natural resources, efforts toward full literacy, reflections on a visit to a newly built hospital, her experience of staying in national-ized hotels, the impact of the United States embargo on Cuba's tourist industry, and observations about the state of the church.

Intriguingly, Day also included some reflections in her article on meeting two exiles from her own country—Rob-ert and Mabel Williams. Robert Williams was from the small town of Monroe, North Carolina. He is remembered today as the first African American civil rights leader who advo-cated for armed resistance against whites, particularly the Ku Klux Klan, in Union County. Williams led the local chapter of the National Association for the Advancement of Colored People for several years until the organization determined that he was too radical. Williams applied for a charter from the National Rifle Association and formed a Black Guard to serve as protection for black citizens of Monroe because of the injustices he witnessed in the crimi-nal justice system of Union County and his experience of violence committed by white supremacists. In 1961, when the Freedom Riders demonstrated in Monroe, they were forced to appeal to the Black Guard for protection after being overwhelmed by an angry mob of KKK. The Black Guard came to their aid and also sheltered a white couple from the anger of black demonstrators. Later, Williams was accused of kidnapping the white couple. Robert, Mabel, and their two children were forced to flee Monroe. Fidel Castro offered them political asylum in Cuba.

The Williams family lived in Havana for five years. He continued to champion civil rights and spread his views through the radio program "Radio Free Dixie" and a pam-phlet titled *The Crusader*. His book *Negroes with Guns* was published in 1962, the same year that Day traveled to Cuba. Williams and his family eventually moved to China, where government officials treated him with high regard. Day evidently kept in touch with Williams for many years. Their friendship witnesses to her support for the civil rights movement. The Williams family was finally able to return to the United States in 1969.

Peace Missions

Much of Day's traveling in the years following WWII could be characterized as taking part in peace missions, whether she was speaking to groups on topics such as the spirituality of the Catholic Worker Movement, conscientious objection and resistance to war and the proliferation of armaments, or advocating for worker's rights. In addition to travel around the United States, she took trips abroad more and more frequently to places such as Africa, Australia, England, India, Italy, and Russia. Her primary aim was to learn as much as she could about the means to make peace in the world and to use her voice to spread a gospel of peace that would inspire others to radically alter their way of life so that all people—regardless of their social class—and the planet itself could flourish.

As noted earlier in this chapter, she built strong alliances with other leaders, both religious and nonreligious, who were working to create a new vision for society by addressing the systemic causes of racism, poverty, and injustice—Ammon Hennacy, Clarence and Florence Jordan, Robert and Mabel Williams among them. As a Catholic, Day believed that the Roman Catholic Church had a distinctive voice to contribute and a special mission to respond to economic disparities, colonialism, racism, and social injustices. The church for her was the place where time and eternity met, human nature had the potential to be transformed, and people were sent out to embody Christ's love in the world.

Two trips that she took to Rome hold a special place of importance among her travels. The first trip was in April 1963 when she joined a pilgrimage of women to Rome. The trip was planned just six months after the opening of the proceedings of the Second Vatican Council, a meeting intended to consider the Roman Catholic Church's role in the modern world. Plans for the "Women's Peace Pilgrimage to Rome" were sparked by Virginia Naeve of Vermont and Alice Pollard of New Hampshire. The pilgrimage was intended as a "means of expressing support, by women from different countries and walks of life, to Pope John for his contributions as a humanitarian and champion of peace. . . . It would represent further a plea and a prayer; an appeal to Pope John in his role as great spiritual leader to call once more upon the world's rulers to withdraw from the nuclear arms race."[19]

The original goal was to get twenty-five women, including Catholics, Protestants, and women from other faith traditions, to join the pilgrimage. More than forty Americans were joined in Rome by women from Japan, Canada, England, Norway, Belgium, Holland, Germany, France, Switzerland, Italy, and Austria. Twenty-nine women departed together on April 20, 1963, from New York and then were joined in Rome by Day and several more women, including Carol Gorgen and Marguerite Tjader Harris. Day's fare was paid for by a donor. All of the women had been heavily involved in peace activist groups and had been recommended by those organizations or by a pastor or priest to participate in the trip.

They carried with them a letter of thanks written to Pope John XXIII for his encyclical *Pacem in Terris*, which they described in the letter as a "step of inestimable significance." The encyclical underscored recent movements for human rights, highlighted the limitations of political leaders to solve the problem of war, and emphasized that peace could not consist in "equality of arms" but had to be based "in mutual trust." Several groups signed the letter to the pope: Women Strike for Peace, Fellowship of Reconciliation, Women's International League for Peace and Freedom, The Catholic Worker, American PAX, and other independent peace workers. Women making the pilgrimage were present at a general audience at the Vatican held on April 24, 1963, where they were publicly thanked by the pope for supporting his stand for peace. Several representatives of the group also traveled to Switzerland, the U.K., Sweden, Canada, and Poland. In Geneva, they were received by UN Secretary-General U Thant, both the U.S. and U.S.S.R. disarmament delegations, and the World Council of Churches (WCC). A letter was shared with the Central Committee of the WCC thanking Dr. W.A. Visser t'Hooft, Dr. Ernest Payne, and Dr. Franklin C. Fry for the WCC's expressions of concern and regret regarding United States hostility toward Cuba. After the trip the women sent out press releases and additional telegrams voicing their opposition to the build-up of nuclear arms, including one to President John F. Kennedy. The women continued to ponder the trip's long-term impact and considered additional ideas for actions that could be taken as a result of their pilgrimage. They suggested that peace women should be represented at upcoming meetings of the Second Vatican Council and to let the pope mediate differences between President Kennedy and Soviet Premier Nikita Khrushchev.[20]

In September 1965, Dorothy traveled with Eileen Egan to Rome for a second time. Egan gained notoriety as more than just a traveling companion for Day later in Dorothy's life. She served as the first staff person for Catholic Relief Services, an organization formed in 1943 to resettle refugees from Europe, Asia, and Latin America. Among others,

Egan helped to found the American PAX Association, the predecessor of PAX Christi. Her association with the Catholic Workers began in the 1960s. While she never lived at the Worker house, Egan was trained as a journalist and made significant contributions to the *Catholic Worker* paper. When Eileen and Dorothy traveled together to Rome in 1965 they went to pray for peace and to observe the proceedings of the Second Vatican Council. They carried with them this time an issue of the *Catholic Worker* that focused on the theme of "The Council and the Bomb." Day and Egan joined eighteen other Catholic women in Rome, all of whom committed to a ten-day fast. The purpose of their fast was to urge the council to "endorse active nonviolence as an appropriate means of struggle for social justice, condemn weapons of mass destruction, and express support for those who refused to do military service."[21] There were efforts made by other people on pilgrimage to Rome at the time to focus the attention of the council on war. Ultimately, the council did make one comment in December 1965 regarding war in the Constitution on the Church in the Modern World that read: "Every act of war directed to the indiscriminate destruction of whole cities or vast areas with their inhabitants is a crime against God and humanity." These were not the last visits to Rome that Day would make or the last peace missions that Day and Egan would take together.

Day traveled again to Rome in 1967 for the International Congress of the Laity. She took a sort of world peace and justice tour in 1970 with Egan where they stopped in Australia, Hong Kong, India, Tanzania, Rome, and England. Their stop in India was particularly memorable. The two women went to Calcutta and met Mother Teresa, who presented Day with a cross worn by the Missionaries of Charity. In 1971, she joined her friend Nina Polcyn on another international adventure, this time to Eastern Europe and Russia.

Confronting Military Action in Vietnam

Historians Anne Klejment and Nancy Roberts observe that "ten years before a mass antiwar movement began to take shape in response to skyrocketing U.S. military involvement in Vietnam, Day was one of a handful of radical pacifists who dared to defy the political and military conventions of the Cold War era."[22] Catholic Workers planned and held educational programs on peace issues at Tivoli, the Worker farm where Dorothy resided after she returned from 1965 until she moved back to the city to live at Maryhouse. Throughout this time, antiwar articles were included in each issue of the paper. Prominent Catholic intellectuals and peace activists shared their views in the *Catholic Worker* paper.

Thomas Merton, the famous Trappist monk and hermit, used the *Catholic Worker* as a vehicle for his writing on racism, peace, and nuclear war. "Chant to Be Used in Processions Around a Site with Furnaces" (July–August 1961), an antiwar poem, was the first piece that Merton published in the paper. By that time, Merton and Day had developed a friendship through letters. They began exchanging letters in 1956 and shared in their letters common interests in "peacemaking, observations about social change, problems in the Catholic Church, obedience and disobedience, the Cold War, community life, marriage, their hopes and frustrations, their current reading, the meaning of love, and a wide range of issues for which advice was sought."[23] Merton and Day were allies and mutually appreciative of each other's work. He supported the Workers and sent gifts of cheese and fruitcake made by monks at the Abbey of Gethsemani. When Merton was censored in the spring of 1962 and ordered not to publish any more of his writings on war and peace, the *Catholic Worker*, a paper run by laity, had the freedom to publish his articles under pseudonyms such as Benedict Monk.

Other noteworthy peace activists such as Daniel and Philip Berrigan regularly contributed articles to the paper. The Berrigan brothers achieved significant acclaim for creating a new form of resistance near the war's end. Philip took part in October 1967 in a draft board raid with a group who came to be known as the Baltimore Four. Both brothers were involved in the Catonsville Nine demonstration in May 1968 in which they, along with seven others, dropped napalm on draft board files held in Catonsville, Maryland.

Klejment and Roberts point to a prophetic article Day wrote for the May 1954 issue of the *Catholic Worker* in which she clearly identified the cause of fighting in Vietnam. She called on her readers to "recognize that is it not Christianity and freedom we are defending, but our possessions."[24] Day investigated United States military involvement and building tensions in the region from a "Catholic sense of values," which, for her, complicated things. Her involvement in the peace movement and active resistance to the Vietnam War must be understood in light of the alternative way of life offered by Christianity.

Her article "Theophane Venard and Ho Chi Minh" tells the story of a French missionary who was ordained in 1852 to serve as a Jesuit missionary in Indo-China. Vénard wrote to his family about the opium trade in the region that had been "foisted on the Chinese by the British for profit."[25] He believed that British and French colonial rule was falsely characterized in French papers: "The governments of today (1852) have become godless and secular. . . . Expediency is the rule."[26] A terrible persecution of Christian missionaries was ongoing. According to Day, Vénard and the bishops of his region had chosen to live in a simple way. They lived in houses made of wood and mud with thatched roofs. The church buildings they constructed were equally rudimentary. Thérèse of Lisieux, the model for the Catholic Workers' understanding and practice of the "little way," viewed Vénard as her "favorite saint." Vénard and other missionaries found themselves in great danger when the French departed from the region in 1860. He was hunted down, imprisoned in a wooden cage, and then beheaded for his work with indigenous people in the area. For Day, the importance of Vénard was that he suffered with the people who had been held captive by colonial powers for the cause of "western materialism."

She pointed out that colonialism affected the way missionaries were viewed and played a significant role in influencing and forming Communist leaders. Ho Chi Minh was educated in France and for some time sought refuge there after his family was jailed in 1911. He later became the organizer of the Intercolonial Union, editor of the paper *Pariah*, one of the founders of the Communist party, and the Communist National Leader of North Vietnam. The same political, social, and economic repression that caused the martyrdom of Vénard also inspired dictators.

We may be wondering at this point about the church's own role in supporting colonial powers. Day was well aware of the role that the Catholic Church played in colonization and critiqued church officials for supporting political and economic oppression. Day argued against both political and religious leaders in the United States who supported the Cold War by saying that the country's military operations in Vietnam were defending freedom. A good example is her dispute with Cardinal Francis Spellman of the Archdiocese of New York. Spellman opposed the Catholic Worker's pacifist stance during the years leading up to WWII. Cardinal Spellman was equally disenchanted with the Catholic

Workers' stance in regard to the Cold War and Vietnam. Dorothy, however, continued to articulate her own view quite clearly: The church offered an alternative vision for a way of life that was governed by the limited perspectives of government leaders, United States interests, and security ensured by military force. Christian faith provided the means to critically examine the limited vision of political, social, and economic power.

It is worth noting that Day's observations as stated here reflect the ferment of a larger theological community. Much of her theology and social and political commentary represent an early prototype[27] of Latin American liberation theology. Similar themes emerge from theological discussions in Latin America regarding the intersection between social, economic, and political oppression, the history of colonization, an emphasis on a "preferential option for the poor," and becoming poor as one engages in the struggle for justice. Consejo Episcopal Latinoamericano (CELAM), or the Latin American Episcopal Conference, was created in 1955 in Rio de Janeiro, Brazil, and became an early player in the formation of liberation theology. The organization pushed the Second Vatican Council to consider taking a more substantive role on social justice issues. Gustavo Gutiérrez, a Peruvian theologian and Dominican priest, is known for coining the term liberation theology in his now classic theological text *A Theology of Liberation* (first published in 1970). The book was written after a historic meeting of Latin American bishops in Medellín, Columbia, in September 1968. *A Theology of Liberation* is Gutiérrez's articulation of the theological backing, support, and fuel for the Latin American movement for liberation. Gutiérrez himself claims that he was naming a movement in Latin America that began in the 1900s. Day identified early on the problems created by United States military action in Latin

America and how that involvement threatened global peace. She wrote, "What nation today is arming its neighbors (in Latin America), intervening in the internal affairs of Europe and Asia, threatening the world peace and security and rapidly surrounding itself with a black curtain of anxiety, suspicion and hatred? The U. S. A."[28]

Klejment and Roberts assert that Day's 1954 article on Vénard and Ho Chi Minh put the *Catholic Worker* on record as taking a pacifist stance in response to United States interests in Vietnam ten years before United States military action in the nation became a major geopolitical issue. She also helped to stoke the interest and prophetic imagination of a new generation of Catholic Workers and thinkers, including people such as Tom Cornell, Thomas Merton, and Philip and Daniel Berrigan. Many of those who identified with the Catholic Worker Movement played key roles in creating peace groups and planning or participating in peace demonstrations throughout the 1960s.

Peace Demonstrations Throughout the 1960s

Tom Cornell became part of the Catholic Worker Movement after picketing the Polaris submarine project in New London, Connecticut with Ammon Hennacy in 1960. Hennacy left the Worker movement at the turn of the new year in 1961 because he said he no longer felt committed to the Catholic Church. Cornell, however, continued working within the movement and participated in or planned several important demonstrations against the war with Vietnam. He protested the persecution of Buddhists by the president of South Vietnam, Ngo Dinh Diem, who was a Catholic. Cornell planned with a larger group of peace activists several draft card burnings. After Congress passed a law in 1965 to broaden draft card violations, Cornell collaborated with others to plan a demonstration in Union Square on November 6. Several well-known activists who had long been allies of pacifist, labor, and civil rights causes were there, including A. J. Muste. Muste was raised in the Dutch Reformed Church and later became a Quaker. He served as executive secretary of the Fellowship of Reconciliation at the beginning of the Cold War and helped the organization spearhead the Congress of Racial Equality. In his retirement, Muste led the Committee for Nonviolent Action and was a close friend to Martin Luther King Jr. When Day was asked to be part of the demonstration in Union Square, she had just returned from her trip to Rome to observe the Second Vatican Council. She gave a brief speech at the demonstration, in which she said,

> I speak as one who is old, and whose whole lifetime has seen the cruelty and hysteria of war in the last half century, but who has also seen, praise God the emerging nations of Africa and Asia and Latin America achieving their own freedom, in some instances with non-violence. Our own country has, through the tens of thousands of the Negro people, shown an example of what a non-violent struggle can achieve. . . . I wish to place myself beside A. J. Muste to show my solidarity of purpose with these young men.[29]

Their demonstration was met with a counter-demonstration across the street in which calls were made to "Give us joy, Bomb Hanoi" and "Burn yourselves, not your cards."

The tragedy was that these peacemakers themselves encountered some violence within their own movement. Three days later, on November 9, 1965, a young Catholic Worker named Roger LaPorte doused himself with kerosene and lit a match. His body was consumed in flames. He died in the hospital a little more than a day later. Self-immolation was part of the larger protest movement in both the United States and Vietnam. Thich Quang Duc was the first to burn himself alive in a street in Saigon to demonstrate against the persecution of fellow Buddhist monks. In the United States, Norman Morrison, a Quaker, set himself aflame in front of the Pentagon building. Morrison was holding his own child at the time.

LaPorte, however, was the first Catholic peace activist to take his own life as a demonstration against the war. His death was disillusioning to Day, other Workers, and many who had allied themselves with a movement that they believed symbolized an alternative way of and for life. Day and other leaders in the Catholic peace movement began to hear from supporters as soon as word spread about LaPorte's death. Thomas Merton was among those who responded quickly and directly to the situation. Merton had been a supporter of the *Catholic Worker* through donations for many years and helped to found the Catholic Peace Fellowship (CPF) in collaboration with Jim Forest, Daniel Berrigan, and John Heidbrink. Merton sent telegrams to Day and to the CPF leadership. His telegram to Dorothy Day said,

> Just heard tragic death of Roger LaPorte. Deeply shocked and concerned about current developments in the peace movement. Will these do grave harm to the cause of peace? Do they represent a right understanding of nonviolence? I think not.[30]

Day wrote a letter to Merton to ease his conscience. Her letter played a significant role in changing Merton's mind. He later made a public statement of support for "acts of defiance" in the face of war that recognized that he was not responsible for any or all of the acts planned by those as part of the Catholic peace movement.

The death of LaPorte and responses of supporters of the movement to it struck a deep emotional chord with Day that caused her to question the "spiritual maturity of the resisters."[31] Day ensured that the Catholic Worker Movement would be firmly rooted in and informed by the traditions and theology of the early church. She drew on and trained others in ancient spiritual disciplines that could provide the means to sustain activists and rich nourishment for the struggle against a culture infatuated with death. But Day and the Catholic Worker Movement as a whole now found itself faced with new forms of cultural ferment in the 1960s and early 1970s, not only the radicalism of some aspects of the antiwar movement, but also the sexual revolution. More attention will be given to issues that emerged for Day in response to the sexual revolution in the next chapter. At this point, it is important to observe that Day and other Workers continued to think about how the antiwar movement fit within a larger spirituality of resistance. Jim Forest observes that Day lamented LaPorte's death but did not judge. She responded to the situation by encouraging more traditional forms of nonviolent war resistance, including picketing and tax resistance.

Undoubtedly, Day and other Catholic workers played an important role in advancing the antiwar movement of the 1960s. One could question, however, whether or not their efforts or those of other peace activists could be considered a success. A peace agreement that would officially end the war in Vietnam was signed in January 1973, but just a year later the United States began sending millions of dollars in aid to South Vietnam with a sizeable portion of that aid designated to build up the military in the region.

Public Protest on Behalf of Workers

Workers' rights were always central to the publication program of the *Catholic Worker*. Between 1965 and 1975 the rights of farm workers were given increased attention in the *Catholic Worker* and other newspapers, among grassroots activists, and by other media outlets around the country. In fact, Day's last experience in jail resulted from her participation in a strike organized by grape pickers at a California farm on August 2, 1973.

Day was particularly attracted to the leadership of a labor organizer in California named Cesar Chavez. Chavez was Mexican-American, a farmer, a labor leader, and a Roman Catholic. He founded the National Farm Workers Association (NFWA) in 1962 with the $1,200 that he had in his personal banking account. By 1964, there were a thousand members in the organization. The NFWA later became known as the United Farm Workers in 1972 when the organization became an official member of the AFL-CIO.

Two key events created a context in which migrant farm laborers could be easily exploited. First, farm workers and seasonal laborers were excluded from the National Labor Relations Act (1936). The NLRA had given most workers, particularly those in factories, the right to join unions and bargain collectively. Second, the United States and Mexican governments created the Bracero Program[32] during World War II that was intended to maintain a steady stream of laborers from Mexico into the United States to ensure the fields could be harvested and to solve labor shortages during the war. The Bracero Program, however, did not end after WWII. The agreement was extended until 1964 to ensure a steady stream of cheap labor to help harvest crops grown in the United States.

Broadcast journalist Edward R. Murrow did much to raise the consciousness of United States residents regarding the plight of migrant farm workers through his work on a documentary called *Harvest of Shame* that was first televised in 1960. Murrow described the migrant farm worker family as a "modern day *Grapes of Wrath*." The farm laborer was the lowest level of any labor group in the United States. Workers and their families were forced to migrate with crops that needed to be harvested. According to Murrow, men, women, and children worked in the fields an average of 136 days a year and made only about $900. Migrant workers were not eligible at that time for unemployment benefits when they were not working. Many of the farms provided housing for the temporary laborers. Whole families of up to nine or ten people lived in a single room, many members even sharing the same bed. In some cases, families were forced to live out of their cars. Few farms provided adequate sanitation facilities during work hours or in their housing facilities. Children not only worked in the fields but also were denied the opportunity to go to school. Historical studies show that "[t]he availability of Braceros held down wages—average farm worker earnings in California rose 41 percent, from $0.85 an hour in 1950 to $1.20 in 1960, while average factory worker earnings rose 63 percent, from $1.60 in 1950 to $2.60 in 1960."[33] Moreover, braceros were sometimes paid even less than other farm workers. Migrants were bused and trucked like cattle to the fields for work with little hope of ever being able to escape from backbreaking labor or a life of poverty.

Chavez advocated for fair pay and challenged people in the United States to think beyond charity for farm workers. He connected his labor organizing with his deep faith and with nonviolent resistance associated with Gandhi's successes in India's struggle for independence from British colonial rule. Of course this held special significance for Day. Chavez refused to speak of the owners of the farms as "enemies" but rather spoke of them as "adversaries." Chavez used the image of Our Lady of Guadalupe (*Nuestra Señora de Guadalupe*) as one of the union's symbols. Many Mexican Catholics attribute the origin of their faith to Our Lady of Guadalupe, who revealed to a man named Juan Diego that Jesus was the Christ. What may be of greater importance is that Mary spoke to Juan Diego in his own language, Náhuatl, rather than in the language of Spanish conquistadors.

Chavez collaborated with other groups, such as the Agricultural Workers Organizing Committee (AWOC), which was composed mainly of Filipinos. The AWOC had successfully gotten a pay raise from farm growers in Delano, California, in 1965. The NFWA merged with the AWOC to form the United Farm Workers Organizing Committee (UFWOC) in 1966. They continued to use strikes (*huelgas*) and consumer boycotts as strategies to create change. Chavez corresponded with Day on several occasions and visited her in New York in 1966. In 1968, Chavez fasted for twenty-five days at Delano as an act of penance for striker violence. Robert Kennedy ended the fast with Chavez when they attended Mass and took Communion there. Day returned the favor by visiting Chavez in May 1969, when she was on a speaking trip in California. Day met with him at his home and noticed pictures of Gandhi and Our Lady of Guadalupe hanging on his wall. During the same visit, Day participated in a memorial Mass held to honor Robert Kennedy on the first anniversary of his assassination. By 1969, there were more than 14 million people across the United States boycotting table grapes. The strength of the consumer boycott enabled the UFWOC to sign historic contracts with grape growers.

Day visited Chavez on at least two additional occasions in 1971 and in 1973. Her visit in 1973 resulted in her last arrest. At that time Day was seventy-five years old. She traveled to California to spend a week at the Institute for the Study of Nonviolence, a school founded by a nonviolent peace activist named Ira Sandperl and folk singer Joan Baez. Day participated in farm workers' strikes on both August 1 and 2. These strikes were of special significance because a California judge had ruled that farm workers were forbidden from striking. Police showed up on both days with guns and billy clubs.

One of the most famous pictures of Day was taken by photographer Bob Fitch. Day, an elderly woman with gray hair and comfortable walking shoes, is calmly sitting on a cane stool looking up into the faces of two police officers. The photo only shows the backs of the police officers, who were both wearing holsters on their belts that contained government-issued billy clubs and guns. Day was arrested and held in prison for eleven days. She and other protestors, including some nuns, organized prayer vigils while they were in jail. Day also wrote a letter to Catholic bishops in the United States describing her prison experience. The charges against the protestors were eventually dropped and Day was released along with other prisoners on August 13. She kept with her a sort of souvenir of the experience—the prison dress that she wore and that had been signed by the women who were with her on the picket lines and in prison.

If one has to be arrested for civil disobedience, could there be a more fitting demonstration for the last jail experience of a woman whose activism was fueled by a sacramental theology and who can be described as a social mystic? As you will remember, Day took Communion daily. Eating the bread, drinking the wine was a daily reminder of those who farmed the food that would eventually be served as the Eucharistic meal. Taking part in a demonstration that would defend the lives and livelihoods of those who toiled in the fields to pick grapes that would be pressed into wine bore profound social and theological significance.

What Outsiders Failed to Understand

For Day, pacifism was not just a movement opposing the government or a protest against laws enforced by the state and decisions made by leaders of civil society. The state itself was far from the centering force of her reality from the time in which she and Maurin founded the Catholic Worker Movement, throughout decades of war, Cold War, and civil rights, and then in her solidarity with farm workers. Pacifism was an alternative way of life. A letter that was sent by the Internal Revenue Service to the Catholic Worker house in New York in April 1972 is symbolic of what so many at that time did not understand about Day or the movement itself. The IRS demanded a payment of nearly $300,000 to settle their debt for unpaid taxes and fines. Jim Forest points out that the IRS bill was suspiciously sent during a period of military escalation in Vietnam and likely linked to the Catholic Worker's pacifist stance and active protest against the war.[34] Beyond the suspicions held by the IRS and the observations made by Forest about them, the letter shows a significant lack of imagination that any other alternative way of living is possible. Living by an ethic of peace meant that Day would free herself from the contaminants of war, racism, and worship of security and material things, center her actions and beliefs in God, witness for peace, and embody Jesus' own love in the world.

CHAPTER SEVEN

Looking at Things as a Woman

After reading Day's story, questions might still linger about how a *woman* born in 1897 could emerge as one of the most important lay leaders among American Catholics in the twentieth century and become the cofounder of a movement that remains influential in the twenty-first century. There is no doubt that gender influenced the roles that women could inhabit when Day was born. Day's father was reluctant to embrace his daughter's passion and talent for journalism. Remember, he was not enthusiastic about women reporters and went so far as to ask his editor friends to discourage Dorothy from becoming a reporter when she was looking for her first job. However, women's roles at the turn of the twentieth century were also changing. Movements for women's suffrage, socialism, labor, and equal rights for women and people of color were like waterways converging together and nearing a force great enough to create a dramatic wave of change. Clearly, Day was swept into these currents of social, cultural, political, and ecclesial ferment, and yet biographers and historians still debate whether or not she should be considered a feminist. Why?

There are several reasons why biographers and historians debate Day's commitment to feminism. Some feminists may question Day's solidarity with women seeking liberation because of her commitment to the church. Suffrage leader Elizabeth Cady Stanton ultimately determined that the Bible and the church were some of the greatest stumbling blocks for women claiming the fullness of their own humanity. The church, however, was the place in which Day found freedom and beauty. Day told an interviewer in 1975 that she thought women's liberation "is too self-centered. It's not geared to the poor but to articulate middle-class women with time on their hands, the ones who have the least to complain about."[1] She also tended to describe women's nature and roles in stereotypical ways. In her March 1948 column *On Pilgrimage*, she reflected on the activity surrounding her grandson Eric's baptism: "Women do love to be most active, it is natural to them, they are most happy in doing that for which they are made, when they are cooking and serving others. They are the nourishers . . ."[2] Contemporary feminist philosophers and theologians might charge Day with essentialism, a philosophical position that holds that women's nature can be defined by a single inherent quality or unchanging essence, such as motherhood, or, in this case, the virtue of care. Essentialist understandings of women's nature deny the way in which women's roles have been created or constructed by sexist attitudes and expectations within society. How many women do you know who would say cooking and serving others is "natural" to them? Aren't these skills cultivated among women through a process of socialization?

Another issue, particularly for feminists, is that later in Day's life and during the 1960s' sexual revolution, she defended traditional Catholic teachings regarding sexual ethics, birth control, and abortion. Day's decision to have an abortion amidst a failing relationship with Lionel Moise in particular is a flashpoint for discussion. This event in Day's life is controversial for both feminists and Roman Catholics, albeit for different reasons. On the one hand, some Catholics question Day's worthiness to be considered for sainthood in light of her decision to have an abortion. The Catholic Church's official teaching is that abortion is a grave evil even if the mother's life is threatened. The majority of feminists, on the other hand, worry that Day later came to adopt and defend the Catholic Church's official stance against abortion and reflected with regret on her decision to abort a child. Most feminists seek to protect women's reproductive freedom and access to abortion, particularly the 1973 Supreme Court decision on Roe vs. Wade.

Day also committed herself to a celibate lifestyle after the end of her common-law marriage with Forster Batterham. She did not understand homosexuality, and her homophobia comes through in some of her writings. Historians and biographers of Day sometimes point out that with regard to homosexuality she was a product of her time. However, there were other religious social activists of Day's generation who took a much more progressive stance on homosexuality; Vida Dutton Scudder was among them.

Perhaps most important for contemporary feminist theologians is the fact that Day did not openly challenge the concept of an exclusively male priesthood. When she had disagreements with church leaders like Cardinal Spellman, she said that she would be obedient to the church first even if it meant the Catholic Worker would have to change its course.

The reasons not to consider Day a feminist laid out above could close the case for her feminism. But it is worth considering two additional questions: Would something significant be missed about the way in which Day's theology and life story are empowering for women if her feminism is only treated in a superficial manner? Would something significant be missed about the variety of expressions of Christian feminism? As you likely recognized in reading this account of her story, Day never predictably fit in any stereotypical boxes as a daughter, a woman, a journalist, an activist, a Roman Catholic, a pacifist, or a mother. June O'Connor, a scholar who has written from a feminist perspective about *The Moral Vision of Dorothy Day*, contends that she accepted "traditional, conventional roles assigned to men and women" and that sexist thought patterns sometimes clouded her moral vision. At the same time, O'Connor thinks there is a "hidden feminist dimension in her thought."[3] The feminist dimension of Day's theology and life comes through clearly in my reading of her story as well.

Feminism at its most basic level is the claim that women are fully human. In practice, feminists look at the world through the experiences of women and insist on a commitment to listening to and advocating for women and all people who have been devalued and pushed to the margins of society. Day's lack of a significant commitment to social movements that worked specifically for the expansion of middle class white women's roles outside the home, women's suffrage, or reproductive freedom does not necessarily exclude her from being considered in line with feminist thought and activism. Day's critique of a white feminist movement for liberation as too closely tied to the agendas of white upper middle class women was articulated later in a similar way in academic theological discussions by womanist theologians such as Jacquelyn Grant. Womanist theology emerged out of the experience of African American women and developed a religious and conceptual framework that articulates the distinctive theological perspectives and moral discernment of women of color. Unlike many other white female leaders in the twentieth century, Day had a sense of how race, gender, and social class intersected in a way that exacerbated women's economic, social, and political oppression. Moreover, she had a strong sense of the experience of women around the globe through extensive travel, the relationships she built with recent immigrants, and her participation in advocacy for farm workers.

A broader range of theological positions exists among those who take the concerns of women and their liberation seriously than is sometimes recognized in histories and studies of Christian theological thought and practice. Most feminists today are conscious of the fact that living as a woman within a patriarchal society and church means entering into a realm of difficult choices. In other words, even when women have the best intentions to challenge gender roles and stereotypes, they can find themselves slipping into them quite unexpectedly. When considering Day's story, it is clear that she did not see challenging stereotypical gender roles and attitudes toward women as her primary goal. Nonetheless, significant aspects of her theology, life, and devotional practice accord with feminist thought and values. She embodied a strong challenge in the context of her time to assumptions about stereotypical and traditional roles women should fulfill.

As cofounder of the Catholic Worker Movement, Day embodied a new norm for Catholic women's lay leadership in the twentieth century. Many women (and men) were drawn to the movement because of her concise analysis of the problems facing society and because of her leadership. Women took leadership roles in the movement as editors of the paper and founders or cofounders of their own houses of hospitality. Day clearly articulated and identified in her writings the connections between race, gender, and social class and how these factors excluded people from the mythological American dream of financial success. The statement that she made to an interviewer in 1975 about women's liberation being "too self-centered" suggests that Day did not align herself with the women's movement because it failed to connect the discrimination and injustices experienced by women to other forms of oppression such as racism and classism.

There are some essential aspects of Day's thought and activism that would be missed if we failed to intentionally put on feminist lenses in our study of her life and work. No

one can deny that Day's theology was an embodied theology that is not separate from her identity as a woman. Her views on sexuality and sexual orientation are not progressive by twenty-first century standards, but the way in which she embodied her beliefs clearly challenged stereotypical gender roles and attitudes regarding women's roles in both the church and society. This chapter will outline the contours of Day's feminism by exploring feminist dimensions of her theology, her early commitment to and consistent alignment with socialist causes, and her understanding of motherhood as nurturing both her own daughter and a larger movement.

Feminist Dimensions of Dorothy Day's Theology

Day was a social mystic formed by a rich tradition of Christian mysticism. Feminist historians think that mysticism for women has in the past been a means of resistance to male dominance and abuse of power within society and the Christian church. Janet Ruffing suggests in her book *Mysticism and Social Transformation* that "mysticism itself has been a source of resistance to woman-negating forces and a source of solidarity with others who suffer the same deprivations and conflicts."[4] Mystical experiences enable individuals to overcome a "too small sense of self," to identify new experiences of Spirit "within the concrete social location of love of neighbor," and symbolize a form of resistance for those of lesser power to the ways in which power is misused by male leaders in church and society.

There are striking similarities between Day's descriptions of her encounters with God and the way medieval women mystics named their experience of and the intimacy they felt in their relationship with God. Remember that Maurin compared Day to Catherine of Siena. Teresa of Avila was

167

one of the namesakes for Day's daughter, Tamar Teresa. Day frequently referenced Teresa's writings in her own work. She preferred personal and relational images of God. Her references to God as lover are very similar to the writings of medieval women mystics like Mechthild of Magdeburg. Day embraced humility while at the same time having a strong sense of authority within the community of faith. These aspects of Day's thought and practice reflect the influence of mysticism and suggest a feminist dimension to the theology that fueled her activism.

Genuine Humility versus "Debasing and Repulsive" Humility

The concept of humility and feminist critiques of it should be considered in greater detail. Women and men throughout Christian history have been asked to imitate the life of Christ by making sacrifices for the sake of others. Traditionally, these sacrifices are seen as a response to the human sins of selfishness and pride. Seeing oneself as part of a community and willingly sacrificing self-interest in light of the common good is central to the Christian narrative. Throughout Christian history women have been lifted up as models of humility both in the church and in society. Men, however, have not always been asked to make the same sacrifices. The notion of "the good Catholic woman" is prominent among Catholics and identifies women with Mary's femininity and humility and her willingness to lay down her own life to bring Christ into the world. Other descriptions of "good" Christian women that associate women with self-sacrifice can be found across denominational lines, including the role of the pastor's wife as it emerged early on in Protestant traditions. Humility as it has played out in the reality of women's lives is deeply problematic for feminist theologians. Where the problem lies is when women are prevented from realizing their own full potential and sacrificed by others for others' sake. Day herself made a clear distinction between genuine humility and "debasing and repulsive" humility.

> One must only be humble from a divine motive, otherwise humility is a debasing and repulsive attitude. To be humble and meek for love of God—that is beautiful . . . but to be humble and meek because your bread and butter depend on it is awful. It is to lose one's sense of human dignity.[5]

Humility cast in this light accords with feminist values.

Today, some feminist theologians distinguish between concepts of genuine humility and false humility. False humility is imposed on someone, can be used as a tool to oppress women (humiliation), and, to draw on Day's words, makes one humble and meek for a god made in the image of the other. Genuine humility is a way of resisting individualism, fosters a connection to community, inspires acts of justice and love, and involves personal and social transformation. Day emphasized the importance of humility in a manner similar to the medieval women mystics. Humility cemented the relationship between love and poverty and created the inward space to live with, among, and as those who were pushed to the margins of society.

There is another way in which Day's understanding of humility should be compared to medieval women mystics. Humility enabled her to achieve and maintain a position of authority within a patriarchal church. Recall Cardinal Spellman's objection to the stance of solidarity that Day took with gravediggers who were striking for better pay in 1949. Exactly two years after the strike ended, Day was summoned to the Archdiocesan Chancery office by Monsignor

Edward Gaffney. She was told that the *Catholic Worker* should cease publication or change its name so as not to be identified as "Catholic." Day responded to Monsignor Gaffney several days later in a letter in which she stated that her first obedience was to the church. She defended her stance of solidarity with the gravediggers and their right to unionize. Day went on to explain that the *Catholic Worker* had been in existence for eighteen years, with a readership of 63,000. They couldn't just cease identifying themselves as Catholic.

The *Catholic Worker* ran articles highlighting the fact that other people involved in writing and editing the paper were against changing the name, appealed for dialogue, and underscored the inconsistencies in the Cardinal's position. There were organizations like Catholic War Veterans using Catholic in their name and yet they were not being held accountable for representing the official views of the Archdiocese in the same way as the *Catholic Worker*. Of course, the Cardinal's own anticommunist opinions were more in line with the Catholic War Veterans. Day pressed this question: Shouldn't the *Catholic Worker* have the same freedom to express its views that is enjoyed by the Catholic War Veterans? Day maintained her willingness to be obedient but ultimately the Archdiocese dropped the matter.

Years later, Day spoke about her relationship with Cardinal Spellman:

> I have my own way of disagreeing with him. Anyway, the point is that he is our chief priest and confessor; he is our spiritual leader of all of us who live here in New York. But he is not our ruler. . . . The Church has never told its flock that they have no rights of their own, that they ought to have no beliefs or loyalties other than those of the Pope or one of his cardinals. No one in the Church can tell me what to

> think about social and political and economic
> questions without getting a tough speech back.[6]

She maintained her humble obedience to the church and clarified her understanding of the spiritual authority of the Cardinal. Day's response bears a feminist dimension because she did not just tacitly accept the authority of the Cardinal. She also clearly maintained a sense of her own authority concerning social, economic, and political issues. Jim Forest observes that she was loyal to the church, but she "never committed herself to instant compliance."[7]

Medieval women mystics such as Teresa of Avila gained a sense of authority in the church not only through direct, intuitive experiences of God but also by appealing to humility. Teresa reformed Carmelite convents during the time of the Inquisition. Questioning established practices of the church at that time would have placed anyone at risk. Humility not only connected one to the life of Christ but also served as a sort of strategy for survival. Some scholars use the term "humility topos" to describe the way in which medieval women mystics appealed to humility. Humility topos is a common rhetorical strategy used by an author who claims to be ignorant or less intelligent in order to be able to ask difficult and sometimes confrontational questions that may open the door to change or transformation. Some feminist historians argue that medieval women mystics exploited humility, a characteristic and virtue identified with women at the time, so that they would be able to bring about much needed changes in the church and society.

Another example can be found in Catherine of Siena. Catherine wrote to Pope Gregory XI during the time in which the papacy was in Avignon and urged him to return to Rome. Catherine began her letter by introducing herself with humility as "[y]our poor unworthy daughter

Catherine, servant and slave of the servants of Jesus Christ," but then continued by challenging the pope to be courageous, not to be afraid, and not to listen to the advice of "evil counselors."[8] Her advice bore implications for both the church and the state. Catherine's advocacy provided the opportunity centuries later for her to be deemed a doctor of the church and for many women to consider her as the prototype of modern women reformers.

We may question whether using humility as a survival strategy that results in women's ability to gain authority in a patriarchal church is passive-aggressive and repressive for women. Many feminist theologians would agree, and this point is well-taken. However, the strength of humility as a voluntary form of resistance must be considered in its own light. Day and the medieval women mystics weren't merely casualties of a tradition defined by men; they clearly forged their own strong identities and shaped communities under their leadership. Humility enabled Day to connect with others, confront male power and authority, and lead alongside others committed to a movement. The concept of genuine humility as opposed to "debasing and repulsive" humility is useful when trying to understand how humility functioned in the writings of some of the medieval women mystics as well as in Day's own consciousness.

Day Honored the Body

Day sometimes quoted Maurin's phrase "Man is spirit, Woman is matter." Feminist philosophers and theologians would be concerned about the sharp distinction between spirit and matter that could be read into this statement. But Day had a more holistic and integrated understanding of the relationship between body and spirit that resonates well with feminist aspirations to honor the creativity associated with women's bodies and claims the fullness of women's humanity.

Caring for the body and the bodies of others enabled Day to experience a profound connection with God and to see herself in interdependence with a larger web of life. Day affirmed the goodness of her body as a way of connecting to others and the mystical body of Christ in a journal entry she made on Valentine's Day in 1944.

> Our dear flesh, our good bodies, which God made, which begin to die even as we begin to live, ever dying, ever renewing and finally decaying and being put into the ground like grains of wheat to rise again with new life at the last day. . . .
>
> But this aging flesh, I love it, I treat it tenderly, but also I rejoice that is has been well used. That was my vocation—a wife and mother, I gave myself to husband and children, my flesh well used, droops, my

breasts sag, my face withers, but my eyes and lips rejoice and love and laugh with happiness.[9]

The image of being a body well used is a powerful one. Praying, reading, writing, editing, meditating, cooking, cleaning, traveling, giving birth, tending the sick, standing on picket lines, and visiting people in prison were all deeply embodied activities that enabled Day to cultivate her life with God and in community.

Christian spirituality expert Stephanie Paulsell in her book *Honoring the Body* reveals the practice as "a vital aspect of Christian spirituality."[10] Paulsell writes,

> Christian conviction about the goodness of the body, coupled with a recognition of the body's vulnerabilities, has nurtured a profound sense of responsibility for the protection and nourishment of bodies through the history of the church.[11]

Some of the devotional practices that emerged in the Middle Ages will be instructive here. Monastic communities and some of the women mystics of the High Middle Ages were influenced by the writings of and devotional practices associated with Bernard of Clairvaux, a Cistercian monk who lived in the twelfth century. Feminist historian Carolyn Walker Bynum points out that Bernard

> [u]ses 'mother' to describe Jesus, Moses, Peter, Paul, prelates in general, abbots in general, and more frequently himself as abbot. To Bernard, the maternal image is almost without exception elaborated not as giving birth or even as conceiving or sheltering in a womb but as nurturing, particularly suckling. Breasts, to Bernard, are a symbol of the pouring out toward others of affectivity or of instruction and almost

invariably suggest to him a discussion of the duties of prelates and abbots.[12]

The writings of several medieval women mystics, such as Julian of Norwich, bear the marks of Bernard's influence.

Julian is well-known among contemporary feminist historians and theologians for her references to God and Jesus as mother. She was an anchoress who lived a cloistered or secluded life in a church in Norwich, England, so that she could devote her attention to prayer for the sake of others. She focused on images of Jesus' suffering as she meditated. Julian lived during the time in which the black plague spread throughout Europe. Jesus' broken body became a fitting symbol of the suffering people, particularly women, faced. Jesus suffered just like the sick, frail broken bodies that had been fraught with disease and then carried throughout the streets for their disposal. Women in particular identified with Jesus' suffering because they had lived through the experience and danger of childbirth only to witness the death of their children due to uncontrollable disease. Their bodies, like Jesus' body, had been used to nourish children of the community. Julian reflected on Jesus' motherhood in her book of *Showings:*

> So Jesus Christ, who opposes good to evil, is our true mother. We have our being from him, where the foundation of motherhood begins, with all the sweet protection of love which endlessly follows.
>
> As truly as God is our Father, so truly is God our mother.[13]

Jesus feeds and nourishes others with his own body like a mother feeds and nourishes a child at her breast. Day referenced another famous quote from Julian's writings on more than one occasion in her column in the *Catholic Worker:*

"He will make everything to turn out well!" The solace offered in Julian's statement must have been a comfort to someone like Day who was so immersed in the sickness and suffering of the world in her own era.

A connection can be made between Day's leadership within houses of hospitality and Bernard of Clairvaux's association of Jesus as mother with the role of abbot. You may wonder why Day wrote about her vocation as a wife and a mother of "children" in her journal entry when she was only married once for a brief time to Berkeley Tobey and was biological mother to only one child. She is drawing here on the images of the church as the bride of Christ and the abbess as mother. Abbots and abbesses in monastic communities assess the needs of the whole, ensure that all needs are met, and attend to the community's spiritual needs. Historically, the abbot or abbess was often a patron for his or her monastic community, held a great deal of power within it, and donated his or her income and property to the monastery.

Of course, Day was not formally or officially placed in the role of abbess as cofounder and member of a movement of lay people. But consider carefully the comments made by some of the Catholic Workers who were interviewed by historian Rosalie Riegle and who worked alongside Dorothy and lived in the New York house of hospitality. Chuck Mattei said, "As the foundress and untitled leader, she brought a certain stability and a certain sense of security and order."[14] Ed Turner recalled that "she ruled the New York house and its attendant farms because she was personally responsible for them. What she said was final."[15] "And so Dorothy would listen," Tom Cornell reflected, "to all the tales coming out of our 'house of hostility,' as Stanley Vishnewski used to call it. Then she'd give admonitions, such as,

'No, no, you can't reject a person like this. Someone else will come in her place, and the devil you have is better than the devil you're going to get.'"[16] Day in some sense may be thought of in the role of mother, of abbess, within the house of hospitality.

God as "Companion, Friend, Lover"

Another intriguing feminist dimension to Day's theology is reflected in her references to God in personal and relational terms such as "companion, friend, and Lover." Day's description of God as lover bears a strong similarity to the writing of the medieval mystic Mechthild of Magdeburg. Mechthild was Beguine, meaning that she lived in a community of women who devoted themselves to a life of prayer but was not part of an official religious order of the Catholic Church. Carolyn Walker Bynum thinks that Mechthild was aware of her femaleness as a positive and negative piece of her identity. Christ's suffering is a central theme in Mechthild's writing. Her devotional practices included meditating on Christ's Sacred Heart. She believed that when one experiences times of feeling separated from God that one suffers in a way that is cleansing. When experiencing union "with God we are ravished in delight."[17] Again, this desire to be close to Christ's suffering and to model oneself on his example is a mark of thirteenth-century spirituality. Mechthild wrote in her book *The Flowing Light of the Godhead*, "The closer I am to the embrace of God, the sweeter is the kiss of God. The more lovingly we both embrace, the more difficult it is for me to depart."[18]

Like Mechthild, Day compared her relationship to God with the intimacy she experienced through human love. "The union between man and woman is the closest analogy in this moral life to the union between God and man. One cannot properly be said to understand the love of God without understanding the deepest fleshly as well as spiritual love between man and woman."[19] What is intriguing to contemplate is the fact that being lost in God's embrace did not lead to self-deprecation for these women but rather to their empowerment.

For Christians who are unfamiliar with the tradition of Christian mysticism, reading about one's relationship with God in terms of "union between a man and a woman" may be uncomfortable. It is not clear whether Day read Mechthild's *Flowing Light of the Godhead.* Day was such an avid reader that it is certainly possible that she encountered Mechthild's writings. There is no doubt that she encountered other writers who identified with the same mystical tradition through retreats that Fr. John Hugo led for Catholic Workers and through his publications. Day quoted one of his publications at length in her column *On Pilgrimage.* Hugo thought that "sexual union and the union of love between God and the soul is at once affirmed by reason and pointed out by divine revelation itself."[20] Similar references to union with God can be found in the mystical writings of John of the Cross and Bernard of Clairvaux. Bernard of Clairvaux closely connected his description of union with God with the biblical book Song of Songs. Bernard spent hours contemplating Song of Songs and wrote more than eighty sermons on the first three chapters alone.

Day's concept of genuine humility, practice of honoring the body, and personal reflections on God as "companion, friend, and Lover" underscore woman-empowering aspects of her thought and represent a feminist dimension of her theology. Her early commitment to and consistent alignment with socialist causes offers another feminist dimension to her thought and practice.

A Socialist Feminist

What is too often missed in the attention that is given to the influences of socialism on Day is the emphasis within socialist movements themselves on rights for workers regardless of race or gender. Neither the Socialist Party nor the Industrial Workers of the World (IWW) would have claimed to be feminist per se, but both advocated for women's suffrage. Women's right to vote was part of the Socialist Party platform. In those states where the Socialist Party was strong, women won the right to vote more quickly. The IWW more clearly recognized the connection between economic injustice and a wide range of injustices than even the Socialist Party. Day covered the work done by the IWW in the years that she served as a reporter for socialist publications. Gender, race, ethnicity, age, and sexuality were linked to social, political, and economic power and control. Day was influenced by these ideas. She once remarked that "the place of sex was as pertinent to questions of social justice as were discussions of war, overpopulation, capital punishment, birth control, abortion, euthanasia, and the role of the state."[21]

Socialism reached the height of its influence in the United States between the years 1897 and 1912. Day grew up and formed her own ideas about the world during the years that socialism gained prominence in the United States and on the global political stage. Socialism as a movement encompassed a range of organizations and groups working for social change. The Socialist Party in the United States was founded in 1897, the year of Dorothy's birth. In 1905, the IWW emerged in opposition to the policies of the American Federation of Labor. Day became involved with this group of socialists, who were known for their radicalism and anarchism. The goal of the IWW was to promote worker solidarity in a revolutionary struggle to overthrow the employing class. Their motto: "An injury to one is an injury to all." By 1910, the "Wobblies" were making a concerted effort to recruit women and black workers through the publication of the leaflet "To Coloured Workingmen and Women."

Some of the most well-known leaders of the socialist movement were associated with the Wobblies, including Eugene Debs and Elizabeth Gurley Flynn. Debs ran for president many times on the Socialist ticket and in 1912 won nearly one million votes. Day would have been about fifteen years old when Debs made his 1912 bid for the presidency. Socialists made significant inroads in Congress by securing the passage of a considerable body of legislation.

Socialists and the Wobblies opposed feminism, but they supported women's suffrage and equal rights for all workers regardless of race or gender. Socialist organizations were some of the first to give women equal voice and vote. The party practiced suffrage for women internationally. As a result, the number of women who identified themselves among the ranks of the socialists increased. Flynn became well-known for her oratorical skills. She gave her first speech at the age of the sixteen on "What Socialism Will Do for Women." Flynn was an active leader in the Lawrence textile strike (1912) and the Paterson silk worker strike (1913) and a founding member of the American Civil Liberties Union. In 1936, Flynn joined the Communist Party and later began writing a feminist column in the *Daily Worker*. She was particularly concerned about women's rights, supported birth control, women's suffrage, and criticized the leadership of trade unions for being male-dominated.

Remember that Day insisted that the paper for the movement she and Maurin cofounded be called the *Catholic Worker*. She chose the title in an intentional effort to attract readers from another paper, the *Daily Worker*. I don't think this was an effort to circumvent the reporting being done by the socialist paper with which Flynn was associated. Rather, Day wanted to be sure to underscore Christian sympathies for the rights of workers. The title also framed the discussion of worker rights in response to Pope Pius XI's statement that workers had been lost to the church. Day hoped the church would take a stronger stance in support of workers' rights.

Day first heard Flynn speak in 1917 when she was assigned to report on a speech that she gave to raise money to help miners on strike in Minnesota. Jim Forest says that she "wept as twenty-seven-year old Flynn described the brutality that was being heaped upon the strikers, the appalling conditions of the mines, and the destitution being suffered by the miners' families."[22] A collection was taken up for the miners and Dorothy gave every last penny she had in her purse. Day's emotional response demonstrates the way in which she identified some common cause with Flynn. Little historical information can be gleaned about a strong relationship between Day and Flynn, but it is reasonable to suggest that the two women remained connected, both personally and through their work. Day referenced a visit she had with Flynn as late as December 28, 1958. Forest also includes in his biography of Day a parenthetical reference to Flynn's bequest of her rocking chair to Day upon her death in 1964. Day wrote an article entitled "Red Roses for Her" in memory of Flynn that was published in the November 1964 issue of the *Catholic Worker*.

Her sympathies with socialist causes and the fair treatment of workers place Day in alignment with many aspects of socialist feminism.[23] She listened to and identified with struggles of working-class women for fair pay, women who experienced life in prison, women overburdened by

addiction, women overwhelmed by caring for their families. Day's reflections on comments she gave in response to a lecture given by Betty Friedan may be the best illustration of her resonance with socialist feminism:

> She spoke also for the middle class, pointing out the technological advances which freed women from drudgery and gave them more time for a public life . . . I could only point to my own experience among the poor and the most recent one of travelling through India and seeing women with baskets and trays of cement and bricks on their heads which they fed in long lines to the men who were working on the bamboo scaffolding around the new buildings going up for housing. . . . The struggle as far as I could see was still a class struggle and the big issue today was world poverty. It is good to think of the way Cesar and Helen Chavez, Jim Drake and his wife work side

by side in the building up of the first Farm Workers' union in the United States.[24]

Most important, Day identified the fullness of Christ's humanity with the experiences of women in living poverty and among those working side-by-side to advocate for economic justice.

Vocation as Mother of a Movement

One final issue needs attention in this exploration of Day's feminism—her vocation of motherhood. Day consistently broke the boundaries of traditional gender stereotypes and norms as they were defined in church and society before the 1960s' sexual revolution by becoming a journalist, choosing to live in community, and living by an ethic of peace. All of these roles were controversial in her time. Perhaps her most controversial role was the way in which she parented her biological daughter, Tamar. In fact, the investment of time Day devoted to the Catholic Worker Movement has led some commentators to characterize her as a less than exemplary mother or to go so far as to suggest that she was a neglectful parent.

Many of the discussions of Day's role as a mother make the mistake of defining the concept of motherhood too narrowly to enable others to wrestle adequately with the variety of commitments and responsibilities that Day navigated. Day viewed her family life as an expression of her commitment to peace. Within the Catholic tradition, the calling or vocation of the family is to transform and renew the earth. The family is a "school of deeper humanity."[25] In other words, families contribute to the building up of communal life and the clarification of the meaning of love within a larger social environment and circumstance. Given Day's commitment to live by

183

an ethic of peace, would it have made sense for her to raise Tamar in a more private family environment that fit with dominant cultural norms? Probably not.

The way Day fulfilled her role as a parent cannot easily be compared to traditional or patriarchal family norms. In his book *All the Way to Heaven: A Theological Refection on Dorothy Day, Peter Maurin, and the Catholic Worker Movement*, Larry Holben says that "Tamar 'took a backseat' to the movement Dorothy co-founded."[26] The assumption that Dorothy could not be a model for parenting if her own biological child "took a backseat" to her social activism is premised on the idea that the needs of biological children must be a mother's primary duty. Day's own story betrays these assumptions. She cut against the grain of traditional norms for motherhood when she chose to have a child out of wedlock and then to intentionally baptize Tamar even when she knew Forster would leave her. Day seemed never to have in her mind the image of herself as a mother invested in developing the private life of a home. She understood her vocation as mother within the context of a larger community and her immense love for her biological child and then later her grandchildren as loves among other loves. Most parents are faced with conflicted loyalties that require one to navigate the tensions felt between living up to one's responsibilities as a parent and other commitments to work, friendship, and self-care. These conflicts and tensions can be particularly acute for women because of expectations of motherhood placed on them by both society and, especially, the church.

Day's writings make it very clear that she loved Tamar. In an article she wrote just after having Tamar she studied the beauty of her newborn baby with a sense of awe and affection:

She sleeps with the placidity of a Mona Lisa so that you cannot see the amazing blue of her eyes which are strangely blank and occasionally ludicrously crossed. What little hair she has is auburn and her eyebrows are golden. Her complexion is a rich tan.[27]

Day's diaries in particular allow her love for Tamar, David, and her adoration for her grandchildren to come through clearly. She made sacrifices just as much as any other parent to make sure that Tamar could leave the city during the summers, fretted over Tamar's marriage to David Hennessy at the tender age of eighteen, and took delight in times when she could babysit her grandchildren. Like any grandmother, she lamented that there were times when she felt like she overstayed her welcome on long visits in the Hennessy home. She helped her daughter pursue a practical degree so that she could provide for her family when David was no longer able to support them.

Day confronted criticism because she chose to raise Tamar in community. She made this entry into her diary on Sunday, September 11, 1938: "I am grieved always of this talk of not raising one's children in these surroundings."[28] Life in community meant being caught up or on some occasions being dragged into the messiness of other people's lives. There is no doubt that life in a house of hospitality presented hardships not faced by families living in their own individual homes. But what is the best way to teach others how to live in community and to live by an ethic of peace? How do you teach your children to live in an alternative way that confronts what Dorothy called the "culture of death"? It is not so easy to do. Christians respond to these questions in a variety of ways. Day's response was to try to live as authentically as possible in a community that provided hospitality for anyone who might have need. Like all parents, she wrestled with her own shortcomings.

Discussions of Day as a mother introduced by historians and biographers all too often focus too much on her relationship with her biological daughter, Tamar. Day's love for her daughter was among other loves and commitments. Isn't this the classic mother's dilemma? More specifically, isn't this the classic feminist dilemma? Day's role as a mother cannot be limited to her relationship with her biological daughter, her son-in-law, grandchildren, or even her parents and siblings. Earlier I compared Dorothy to an abbess as the mother of a monastic community. Day "mothered" a movement as she mentored men and women and in the steadfastness of her nonviolent approach to her work in the family, church, and society.

One of the most poignant examples of this is the way that Day cared for Nanette, Forster's common-law wife and lover after his relationship with Dorothy ended. Forster and Nanette entered into a committed relationship in 1929. Years later, when Nanette was stricken with cancer, Forster asked Dorothy to care for her. This request would be too much for many women, but Day had committed herself to hospitality, love, and peace. She welcomed Nanette into the house of hospitality and tended her as she was dying. Nanette, like Forster, was not religious. Dorothy did not aggressively try to convert her, but her hospitality and prayers were as good as any testimony to deep faith. Nanette was baptized before she died.

Concluding Comments

Day's preference for personal and relational images of God, embodied theology, the way in which she embodied a new norm for the lay leadership among Roman Catholic women, and her vocation as mother of a movement clearly illustrate feminist dimensions of her thought, faith, and practice. Pulitzer-prize winning author and journalist Garry Wills likens Dorothy Day to a "Catholic earth mother," a fitting description to leave with as we consider the relevance of her story for our own lives.[29] The earth mother, Gaia, is a symbol from ancient Greek mythology of a goddess who is born from a Chaos known in the great emptiness of the universe. Gaia's sibling Eros is born with her. Gaia is tremendously fertile and creative. She gives birth to the sea and the sky without the help of a male mate. Day was a lover and mother with an intense love for her own daughter and closest kin and with love abundant enough to give birth to a movement. Her conscience could not rest until those who were submerged into poverty felt the creative love of God in the midst of the chaos of their world.

CHAPTER EIGHT

A Personal Postscript: Dorothy Day's Legacy for Contemporary Christians

Today there are 208 Catholic Worker communities in the United States and 25 houses located in different countries around the world—Belgium, Canada, Germany, Great Britain, Mexico, New Zealand, Sweden, the Netherlands, and Uganda. There is a great deal of diversity in the ways that Catholic Worker communities organize themselves, express their commitment to communal life, and embody an ethic of peace. Dorothy Day left an invaluable legacy to the Catholic Worker Movement as a whole that allowed for great breadth and depth of interpretation in response to the needs of those forming communities within specific local contexts. We are now living in a time when many people of faith are seeking a greater sense of moral coherence and asking how they can live out their faith with integrity and authenticity—as Catholics, Presbyterians, Baptists, Pentecostals, Mennonites, Methodists, Church of the Brethren, and more. Faithful people are increasingly conscious of the disconnect between belief systems that foster a sense of community, belonging, and other-centeredness and a capitalist economic system that is driven by competition, stresses forms of wealth creation that accelerate vast divisions in wealth and exacerbate inequality, and allows so many people and our planet to be seen as reasonable collateral damage in the pursuit of individual wealth. There is a growing fascination with the Catholic Worker Movement among young adults who claim no allegiance to an institutional faith tradition at all but express their resistance to what Day called the "culture of death" by forming intentional communities covenanting together to focus on compassion and building relationships across lines of difference. Day, a woman who lived a life that was integrated and disarmingly authentic, remains a prophetic voice able to speak directly into our context.

However, I must admit that some questions still linger as we near the end of this book. How is Dorothy Day's story relevant for contemporary Christians who are religious social activists of a very different type? I am referring to those people of faith who are never likely to make the commitment to communal life, will continue to work salaried jobs, canvas for political campaigns, and may never choose to be tax resisters. It is clear to me that her story demands a response. But what does her story call those of us to do who have some differences in social location and translation of Christian thought and practices from our own faith traditions? How can we join in the movement she cofounded and inspired?

I took the opportunity to visit several Catholic Worker houses in the United States as I was writing this book and searching for some answers to these questions. Two visits to Maryhouse in New York City, including a conversation with Martha Hennessy, Day's granddaughter, and an afternoon spent with Eduard Loring and Murphy Davis, cofounders of the Open Door Community in Atlanta, Georgia, bore some special significance in my quest.

Day lived the last five years of her life at Maryhouse. However, her experience of living in intentional community spanned forty-seven years. Maryhouse continues to be a women's community and is located near St. Joseph House, a community for men on East 1st Street. The church where Day took Communion on a daily basis is located on the block in between the two Catholic Worker houses.

My first trip to Maryhouse was a kind of pilgrimage after immersing myself in Day's story. I felt the need to see where she lived after entering into conversation with colleagues about her life, consulting with some of Day's own friends, and reading hundreds of pages of books and articles that were either written by her own pen or by her co-laborers and admirers. I went to Maryhouse with my camera in hand so that I would be prepared to capture on film impressions of life in a house of hospitality. A Worker who lived in St. Joseph House welcomed me into the foyer of Maryhouse. He happened to be there on that day to fold the monthly edition of the paper. He greeted me with the warmth and hospitality of a Catholic Worker as I entered.

The building was clearly showing its age. At that time, large strips of paint were peeling away from the walls and deep black grooves were worn into the steps that led into the main room on the second floor. I shrugged off my coat and the bag that I was carrying and eagerly asked my host if I could take some pictures. The Worker who met me at the door reminded me that Maryhouse was just a house, a place where people lived, and taking pictures could be an intrusion into the safety of their space. We talked for about an hour, and he showed me the public spaces in the building and walked with me to St. Joseph House, where I saw the dining room. Just before I left he introduced me to another Worker, a woman who lived there. She was on her way to an appointment but paused to greet me and lamented the fact that I could not stay longer. I mentioned to her my work on this book and she quickly retorted: "We all don't live like Catholic Workers, we just write books about them." She caught the harshness of her tone after making the remark and said, "Well, I don't mean to say that is what you are doing."

The overinflated enthusiasm that I had felt about Day's story was quickly deflated by the sharpness of her comment. Her honesty abruptly, and justly I might add, broke through the facade of my good intentions and scholarly curiosity. I realized that I was absolutely guilty as charged. At the moment that I stood facing two people who devoted their lives to communal living, shared their resources in common, and lived by an ethic of peace, I came face-to-face with the reality that I was really an accidental activist and a "slumdog" tourist.

I have served on a number of advocacy committees within my own church and for national and ecumenical organizations, worked in paid and volunteer leadership roles in social organizations (religious and nonreligious), taught and embraced theologies from the margins, and worshiped in a church for six years that expressed its mission through intentional communities bound together by common cause. However, I have always fallen far short when making a commitment myself to living in the chaotic and volcanic atmosphere of a house of hospitality or holding my possessions in common with a larger community and giving most of them away to people living in poverty. In sum, I have always fallen short of renouncing that middle class privilege from which I have greatly benefited in my life. Those two great witnesses to a movement and to this justice-oriented faith stood as a mirror into my own personal commitments. That meeting pressed me to recognize that I could no longer simply study Dorothy Day. I realized that to know the true story meant I had to immerse myself in it, to enter into my own process of conversion, confront the questions Day's life raised for me about my own activism, and make some new form of commitment.

Day brought together spirituality and social justice in a way that is not often seen even among religious social activists. Practicing a daily rule in the spirit of Benedict established the rhythm of her life. Dorothy herself never felt at home in a cloistered setting but found a daily rule empowering within the house of hospitality that she lived. She referred to her rule on different occasions in her diaries. More traditional practices were included in her daily rule, such as praying each morning and not just quickly "rushing off," reading the Bible (particularly the Psalms and the Gospels) and the "Divine Office" (a recitation of prayers not including the Mass) whenever possible, taking fifteen minutes for quiet around midday, celebrating the Eucharist, writing in her journal, engaging in manual labor, and practicing a nightly examen of conscience. Talking to God rather than reading or talking too much about God, avoiding discussion of what she perceived to be problematic personality traits of other people, continually challenging herself to learn about issues of injustice in the United States and around the world, and encountering people who live on the margins of society were also more novel aspects of Day's daily regimen. One of the most powerful aspects of her story is the way in which she renounced her own privilege and eliminated social and political artifices society had placed between people. It is worth emphasizing that Day didn't just encounter people living in poverty as "clients" of a social service organization. She looked people in the eye and learned to appreciate the essence of their beauty even when it was not easily recognized on the surface.

I adopted as many of these practices as possible when I was on sabbatical and as I was writing this book. These practices enabled me to answer some of the questions about what I personally could do. Developing my own daily rule increased my understanding of Day's principled commitments, struggles, causes, and personal disappointments. Each day, I read one of the Psalms, examined my conscience, avoided making negative statements about others as much as possible, took Communion when I was able, experienced all forms of work (especially manual labor), and observed fifteen minutes of silence at midday. Taking Communion every day was not always possible for a Presbyterian, and I lament this fact. Many Reformed churches still practice Communion only on a quarterly basis, serving tiny crusts of bread and thimbles full of wine. Communion should create the longing to satisfy the hunger of the three billion people in the world today who live in poverty. Remember the description of Fritz Eichenberg's picture of "Christ of the Soup Kitchen." Sometimes there seems to be hardly enough bread and grape juice to whet one's appetite to experience the fullness of worship much less the foretaste of the banquet that Christ set for us. I would also be dishonest if I didn't admit that talking more to God than about God was difficult for a professor. Nonetheless, these practices deepened my understanding of Day and, somewhat surprisingly, taught me new lessons about my connection to a much larger body of people and my relationship to and within a much broader community of faith. Through these practices I discovered the importance of eliminating social distance and explored the meaning of the "little way." The concept of the "little way" awakened within me a greater sense of Day's fearlessness and love for others. Day learned to contemplate God's presence in the midst of daily activities—over the kitchen sink, while bathing her daughter or grandchildren, during annoying interruptions to address the needs of others.

If some similar questions were raised in your mind about your own commitment to embodying love and justice in community as you read about Day's story and theology, I invite you to consider creating your own daily rule. Draw on the wisdom and depth of resources offered by a wide variety of Christian traditions, even those outside your faith tradition, as you create your own rule. Learn to examine your motivations and practice your daily rule for at least a few months.

Creating my own daily rule offered a satisfying response to some of the more personal questions remaining in my own mind, but what about religious social activists coming from a different denominational tradition? A visit to another Catholic Worker community, the Open Door in Atlanta, Georgia, helped me cross another boundary and deepened my reflection on the synergy possible between my own Reformed faith and the Catholic Worker Movement.

Two Presbyterian ministers, Eduard Loring and Murphy Davis, founded the Open Door in the 1980s. Their story is filled with intrigue and conviction. I visited with Loring and Davis one afternoon in their apartment on the second floor of the Open Door and talked with them specifically about why they as two Presbyterian ministers, Christians firmly rooted in Reformed tradition, wanted to start a Catholic Worker community. I was aware of a joke among those in the movement that "you don't have to be Catholic and you don't have to be a worker" to take part but wondered what the Catholic Worker model satisfied that the Presbyterian tradition could not. Loring's and Davis's responses and observations about the contemporary church and world were eye-openers.

Both Loring and Davis hold advanced degrees from some of the finest theological institutions in the United States and have engaged in and led justice-oriented ministries for decades as teachers, pastors, and social activists. Like Day, they are theologians with "street cred." They earned their street cred after visiting Maryhouse and coming to terms with Day's story. In our conversation I discovered that Loring taught at Columbia Presbyterian Theological Seminary for four years. Through a long process of reflection, Loring concluded that Christian activists in today's world have to engage a fundamental existential question: How do we *live* together?

Evidence abounds to suggest the contemporary relevance of Loring's question. Regrettably, the twenty-first century has seen little if any progress concerning disparities in wealth and income. Contemporary historians compare the economic climate and wealth divide of the late nineteenth and early twentieth century to what we are experiencing today. We have made some advances in our understanding of the role that race and gender play in increasing the way our society separates the "haves" from the "have-nots," and yet the gap keeps widening. Labor economist Richard Freeman uses the term "economic apartheid" to describe the contemporary wealth divide in the United States. As this book was being written, the

Occupy Wall Street movement was at its peak and the divisions of wealth illustrated by the percentages of 99 and 1 made their way easily into quips on Facebook and casual conversation. Of course, the 99 and 1 were less relevant to the global economic context where 95 percent of the world's people still live on less than $49 a day (the United States poverty line). According to the 2012 U.S. Census, there are 46.5 million people living in poverty in the United States. The National Coalition for the Homeless estimates that there are 3.5 million people who are homeless (39 percent of them are children). Homeless statistics don't account for many of those who live in temporary or unstable housing: living in a car, sleeping on someone's couch, staying with friends. Hispanic and African American people in the United States are disproportionately affected by poverty in relation to their overall representation in the population. The United States has the highest incarceration rate of all the wealthy, industrialized nations. There are about 2.3 million people behind bars. According to the NAACP, African Americans and Hispanics accounted for 58 percent of all prisoners in 2008 even though these two groups make up only about 25 percent of the total population. Much more could be written here about the problems we are facing as a nation, but I hope you get the point that the statistics tell us that we still don't live together very well.

Ed Loring's and Murphy Davis's own pilgrimage to Maryhouse was their "holy ghost" experience, one that called them to envision a new way of living well with others. They were clear in our conversation that this is a distinctive challenge for Presbyterians and used the PC(USA) as an example because it is the church in which they are both ministers. Connections could be made, however, to other mainline denominations. Loring and Davis are all too aware that local congregations evidence the same social stratification, boundaries, attitudes, and restrictions as our society.

The PC(USA), a denomination formed in 1983 by the merger of the PC(US) "southern stream" and UPCUSA "northern stream," remains the richest per capita denomination in the United States. One of the key issues Loring raised in our conversation was the fact that there was very little constituency within the PC(USA) among people living in poverty. That has been true for mainline white denominations at least since the turn of the twentieth century and continues to be true for the PC(USA) today. What then does that mean for the way we must hear and preach good news to the poor, the central message of our faith? How do Presbyterians live a gospel that speaks out against oppression and challenges Christians to become poor and to eliminate artificial social distance created by human-made institutions?

What Loring and Davis discovered at Maryhouse was the charism of a community knit together by the fabric of their humanity. Catholic Workers embrace and live a way of life based on hospitality, justice, eliminating social distance, and making a preferential option for the poor. Catholic Workers hold onto the awareness that within Christian community there must be a critique of privilege. In community, it doesn't matter if Loring and Murphy are even Catholic in the sense of the Roman church. What matters most is that they are catholic with a little "c," in the universal sense. They both identify themselves with a universal Christian tradition that makes a preferential option for the poor and understands that people are connected by their common humanity (that is, the image of God).

For Loring and Davis, the preferential option for the poor has to be identified within the context in which one lives. There is no way in the context of the southeastern

United States to commit oneself to a preferential option for the poor and avoid the problem of racial discrimination. A ministry to death row inmates, most of them African American, and advocacy work to abolish the death penalty is central to the charism of their community. Loring and Davis have maintained a commitment to a Reformed understanding of the importance of engagement in the public forum and serve as teaching elders, but they also hold goods common and practice a different model of church in which footwashing and Communion hold a central place in ritual. The Open Door, like Maryhouse, is supported by the contributions, conviction, and commitment of the many people. Loring and Davis mentioned that on occasion, sometimes even once a month, the Open Door receives a donation sent to them by the men whom they support on death row. The box usually includes toiletries to be shared with people who are homeless and come to take a shower at the Open Door or live in the house. What a powerful testimony to the synergy possible by working across all sorts of social and class boundaries to really engage the question of how we can live together well. Men and women on death row, whose bodies are locked up and contained far out of the immediate line of sight for the majority of people in our society, are the witnesses to hospitality. They claim their place among a larger body of people by offering compassion, identifying with people who are homeless, and honoring the full humanity of those who don't live behind bars and yet still remain invisible.

Just before I completed this book I paid one more visit to Maryhouse, where I came face-to-face with one of Day's most important legacies: the seventh of her nine grandchildren, Martha Hennessy. When I arrived I found Hennessy in the kitchen cooking for the noonday meal. We talked for about an hour and a half and were interrupted on occasion as other workers entered the kitchen to take part in preparing the meal. Most of the kitchen help that day were college students from Notre Dame who were living at the house as interns for the summer. In the conversation, I was able to ask Hennessy directly what she would say to religious social activists who do not make the commitment to communal life. Hennessy herself is a committed activist who took two trips to Afghanistan as a testimony to the absurdity of recent wars. She shares her grandmother's pacifist commitments. Taking part in political protests has also been part of her activism and witness. Hennessy has been arrested many times for her involvement in political protests. She was surprisingly honest about the fact that she hasn't always regularly attended church or played an active role in the Catholic Worker Movement. I asked her why she fell away from the church for some time. Some of the reasons were practical; when she was a child her family lived in a rural area in Vermont. After her father, David, left the family, Tamar found it difficult to care for nine children and attend church on a regular basis. Martha is also a trained occupational therapist. She has her own family and they live on the same land in Vermont. The busyness of her working life and raising a family of her own kept her out of the movement for a while. There were some theological reasons as well, including the whole concept of original sin and the idea that human beings aren't created good by nature kept her out of the church. She observed that she grew up with "the idea of the dying of the self, personal sacrifice." Both her mother and grandmother "beautifully participated in that life." But, it took quite some time for Martha to "understand what that meant."

I asked her: What drew you back in to the church and the Catholic Worker Movement? She quickly replied, "God and granny." Her return to the Church was influenced by the horrific images of torture coming out of Abu Ghraib during the occupation. The air raid drill protests staged by Catholic Workers in the 1950s are for her a clear example of how activism is attached to difficult real life problems of our culture. She began getting involved in 2004, twenty-four years after attending her grandmother's funeral at Maryhouse. Martha said, "I was always struggling with the paradox of living in a competitive society and yet knowing it is in the connection to community in which you find sustenance. God gives us enough." She found a greater sense of integration at the house of hospitality. She continued to explain that "at the Catholic Worker everyone contributes according to his or her own ability. We all come with different needs, different abilities, different vocations. Everyone who comes has a need."

At this point in our conversation, I turned to one of the student interns, a young woman in her twenties named Abbey Santanello, who had been artfully chopping tomatoes, peppers, and romaine lettuce for a salad and asked her why she wanted to spend the summer there. What did she need from or hope to gain by living at Maryhouse? Santanello replied, "I wanted to gain a deeper understanding of my vocation from a different view and see how compassion plays a part in life." Santanello intends to go to medical school but already at this point in her life she is aware that there is more to one's vocation than just getting a paycheck and caring for one's own. Through daily discipline, intentional focus on community, and the awareness that each of us has something to give we begin to "see the value in each other," Hennessy said. Seeing the value in each other and the way social, economic, and political systems cloud our vision of that is what "makes for the kingdom of God."

Catholic theologian Henri de Lubac once wrote,

> It is not the proper duty of Christianity to form leaders—that is, builders of the temporal. . . . Christianity must generate saints—that is, to witness to the eternal . . . [the saint] is one who succeeds in giving us at least a glimpse of eternity despite the thick opacity of time.[1]

The challenge of witnessing to the eternal in the thick opacity of time is set before all of us, even accidental activists, by Day and those within the contemporary Catholic Worker Movement. All of us won't be able to bring about some great temporal achievement, but we can live in a way that embodies holiness, compassion, and love in the messiness of time. Embodying holiness in time doesn't mean that we won't have rough edges. Friends of Day point out that she had rough edges too. Early in her life, Dorothy Day described herself as an "anarchist." Later she adopted the term "personalist." Now the Roman Catholic Church has entered into the process of canonizing her. Her story compels us to resist the competitive, self-interested assumptions on which our society is organized and based so that we can embody God's presence in the midst of our time. When considered collectively, our countless individual choices have the potential to eliminate poverty and make it easier for all people to feed, clothe, and shelter themselves. In this way, we can take part in a movement and play an essential role in creating a society where it is easier for people to be good.

Author's Note: If you are interested in learning more about Dorothy Day, an archive of the *Catholic Worker* is easily accessed online by visiting www.catholicworker.org.

The website also includes a directory of contemporary Catholic Worker communities. Some communities have their own websites. To visit the website for The Open Door go to http://opendoorcommunity.org/.

Notes

Introduction

1. Philip Kennedy, "Dorothy Day: 1897–1980," *Twentieth Century Theologians* (London: I.B. Tauris, 2010), 118.
2. See Elizabeth A. Johnson, *Friends of God and Prophets: A Feminist Theological Reading of the Communion of Saints* (New York: Continuum, 1998).

Chapter 1: Growing to See the World in a New Way

1. June O'Connor, "Dorothy Day's Christian Conversion," *Journal of Religious Ethics* 18 (Spring 1990): 159.
2. Dorothy Day, *The Long Loneliness: The Autobiography of Dorothy Day* (New York: Harper & Brothers, 1952), 17.
3. Dorothy Day, *From Union Square to Rome* (New York: Arno Press, 1978 [c1938]), 20.
4. I am indebted to historian William Miller for the observations he has made regarding Day's memory and appreciation of her grandfather. See Miller, *Dorothy Day* (San Francisco: Harper & Row, 1982), 3.
5. Ibid.
6. *The Long Loneliness,* 26.
7. *From Union Square to Rome,* 19.
8. *The Long Loneliness,* 21.
9. *From Union Square to Rome,* 24.
10. Ibid.
11. *The Long Loneliness,* 25.
12. *From Union Square to Rome,* 33.
13. Ibid., 31–32.
14. Ibid., 36.

15. Miller, *Dorothy Day,* 20.
16. *From Union Square to Rome,* 28.
17. As quoted by Philip Kennedy in *Twentieth Century Theologians: A New Introduction to Modern Christian Thought* (London; New York: I. B. Tauris, 2010), 117.
18. O'Connor, "Day's Christian Conversion," 161.
19. *From Union Square to Rome,* 42.
20. Ibid., 50.
21. *The Long Loneliness,* 50.
22. *From Union Square to Rome,* 63–64.
23. Ibid., 67.
24. Ibid., 73.
25. Ibid., 86.
26. A memorial is currently being planned to pay tribute to the suffragists. Features of the memorial will include entrance gates depicting the White House gates where the women protestors gathered. For more information, go to http://www.suffragistmemorial.org/.
27. *From Union Square to Rome,* 93.
28. Dorothy Day, *The Eleventh Virgin* (New York: A. & C. Boni, 1924), 260.
29. Jim Forest, *All Is Grace: A Biography of Dorothy Day.* (Maryknoll, NY: Orbis Books, 2011), 59.
30. *The Long Loneliness,* 104.
31. Dorothy Day, "A Human Document," *The Sign* 12 (November 1932): 224.
32. Ibid.
33. *The Long Loneliness,* 134.
34. Ibid., 135.
35. Ibid., 147.
36. Letter from Dorothy to Forster dated September 16, 1929. Robert Ellsberg, ed., *All the Way to Heaven: The Selected Letters of Dorothy Day* (Milwaukee, WI: Marquette University Press, 2010), 28.
37. *The Long Loneliness,* 150.
38. O'Connor, "Day's Christian Conversion," 170.

Chapter 2: Synergy

1. Dorothy Day, with Francis J. Sicius, *Peter Maurin: Apostle to the World* (Maryknoll, NY: Orbis Books, 2004), 40.
2. Day, *The Long Loneliness*, 166.
3. Ibid., 169.
4. See "Mass Exodus from the Plains," no date, http://www.pbs.org/wgbh/americanexperience/features/general-article/dustbowl-mass-exodus-plains/.
5. Hugh Rockhoff, "Great Fortunes of the Gilded Age," National Bureau of Economic Research Working Paper Series, Cambridge: NBER (December 2008), 5.
6. See "The Wealthiest Americans Ever," *New York Times*, July 15, 2007, http://www.nytimes.com/ref/business/20070715_GILDED_GRAPHIC.html#.
7. Day, Sicius, *Peter Maurin: Apostle*, 29.
8. Joseph Brieg, "Apostle on the Bum," The *Commonweal*, April 29, 1939, 10.
9. Day, Sicius, *Peter Maurin: Apostle*, 35–36.
10. Anne Klejment, "Introduction," *Dorothy Day and the Catholic Worker: A Bibliography and Index*, ed. Anne and Alice Klejment (New York: Garland Publishing, 1986), xxiii.

Chapter 3: A Three-Pronged Program of Action

1. Jim Forest, *All Is Grace* (Maryknoll, NY: Orbis Press, 2011), 321.
2. Robert Ellsberg, ed., *All the Way to Heaven: Selected Letters of Dorothy Day* (Milwaukee, WI: Marquette University Press, 2010), 137.
3. Dorothy Day, *House of Hospitality* (New York: Sheed & Ward, 1939, out of print), 25, http://www.catholicworker.org/dorothyday/daytext.cfm?TextID=3.
4. June O'Connor, *The Moral Vision of Dorothy Day* (New York: Crossroad, 1991), 32.
5. Forest, *All Is Grace*, 126.
6. Gordon M. Fisher, "From Hunter to Orshansky: An Overview of (Unofficial) Poverty Lines in the United States from

1904 to 1965—SUMMARY," http://aspe.hhs.gov/poverty/papers/htrssmiv.htm.

7. "Day by Day" column, *Catholic Worker*, March 1934, 5.

8. Dorothy Day, "Valiant Is the Word," *Catholic Worker*, March 1938, 2, http://www.catholicworker.org/dorothyday/Reprint2.cfm?TextID=332.

9. *House of Hospitality*, 39.

10. Ibid., 47.

11. "Day by Day," *Catholic Worker* June 1, 1934, 7.

12. *House of Hospitality*, 44.

13. Rosalie G. Riegle, *Dorothy Day: Portraits by Those Who Knew Her* (Maryknoll, NY: Orbis Books, 2003), 3.

14. *House of Hospitality*, 149.

15. Letter to the editor by John C. Paisley, *Catholic Worker* 6, no. 8 (February 1939): 5.

16. *House of Hospitality*, 240.

17. Dorothy Day, with Francis J. Sicius, *Peter Maurin: Apostle to the World* (Maryknoll, NY: Orbis Books, 2004), 133.

18. Forest, *All Is Grace*, 144.

19. Riegle, *Day: Portraits*, 39.

20. As quoted by Mark and Louise Zwick, *The Catholic Worker Movement: Intellectual and Spiritual Origins* (New York: Paulist Press, 2005), 60.

Chapter 4: A Social Mystic

1. Bradley P. Holt, *Thirsty for God* (Minneapolis: Fortress Press, 2005), 69.

2. Ursula King, *Christian Mystics: Their Lives and Legacies Throughout the Ages* (Mahwah, NJ: Hidden Spring, 2001), 49.

3. Holt, *Thirsty for God*, 75.

4. Conference Program, "Main Currents of Christian Social Thought and Action Today," Adelynrood, South Byfield, MA, August 10–14, 1939. Program enclosed in letter from Gwendolyn Miles to Day dated June 24, 1939. Dorothy Day Archives, Marquette University.

5. Howard Thurman, "Mysticism and Social Action," *The A.M.E. Zion Quarterly* 92, no. 3 (October 1980): 6.

6. Ibid.

7. Walter Rauschenbusch, *A Theology for the Social Gospel* (Louisville, KY: Westminster John Knox Press, 1997; reprint of 1917 ed.), 103–4.

8. Reinhold Niebuhr, *The Nature and Destiny of Man, Vol. II* (New York: Charles Scribner's Sons, 1964; reprint of 1943 ed.), 11.

9. As quoted in Fritz Eichenberg, *Works of Mercy*, ed. Robert Ellsberg (Maryknoll, NY: Orbis, 1992: Orbis, 2004), 84.

10. *House of Hospitality*, 3.

11. Thurman, "Mysticism and Social Action," 9.

12. Dorothy Day, *The Duty of Delight: The Diaries of Dorothy Day*, ed. Robert Ellsberg (Milwaukee, WI: Marquette University Press, 2008), 73.

13. Ibid., 487.

14. Dorothy Day, *By Little and By Little: The Selected Writings of Dorothy Day*, ed. Robert Ellsberg (New York: Alfred A. Knopf, 1983, 2005), 109–111, http://cwx.prenhall.com/bookbind/pubbooks/kagan3/medialib/chapter31/31.htm.

15. *The Duty of Delight*, 43.

16. David Scott, "More than a Feminist," http://davidscottwritings.com/oconnormoralvision/; originally published in *Commonweal*, March 13, 1992.

17. Dorothy Day, *Therese* (Notre Dame, IN: Fides, 1960), viii.

18. King, *Christian Mystics*, 223.

19. Carole Lee Flinders, *Enduring Grace* (San Francisco: Harper One, 1993), 209.

20. As quoted by Flinders, *Enduring Grace*, 210.

21. Ibid., 212.

22. Niebuhr, *The Nature and Destiny of Man*, 254.

23. Dorothy Day, "Room For Christ," *Catholic Worker*, December 1945, 2, http://www.catholicworker.org/dorothyday/Reprint2.cfm?TextID=416.

24. Dorothy Day, *Dorothy Day: Selected Writings,* ed. and with introduction by Robert Ellsberg (Maryknoll, NY: Orbis Books, 2009), 97–98.

Chapter 5: Living by an Ethic of Peace in a Culture Invested in War and Death

1. "Making the World 'Safe for Democracy': Woodrow Wilson Asks for War," History Matters: U.S. Survey Course on the Web created by the American Social History Project / Center for Media and Learning (Graduate Center, CUNY) and the Roy Rosenzweig Center for History and New Media (George Mason University), http://historymatters.gmu.edu/d/4943/.
2. Anne Klejment, "The Radical Origins of Catholic Pacifism: Dorothy Day and the Lyrical Left During World War I," in *American Catholic Pacifism: Dorothy Day and the Catholic Worker Movement,* ed. Anne Klejment and Nancy L. Roberts (Westport, CT: Praeger, 1996), 16.
3. Rosalie Riegle, *Dorothy Day: Portraits by Those Who Knew Her* (Maryknoll, NY: Orbis Books, 2003), 43.
4. Dorothy Day, "What Do the Simple Folk Do?" *Catholic Worker,* May 1978, 5, 8, http://dorothyday.catholicworker.org/articles/587.html.
5. Dorothy Day, "Why Write about Strife and Violence?" *Catholic Worker,* June 1934, 1, 2, http://dorothyday.catholicworker.org/articles/279.html.
6. Riegle, *Dorothy Day: Portraits,* 63.
7. *By Little and By Little: The Selected Writings of Dorothy Day,* ed. Robert Ellsberg (New York: Alfred A. Knopf, 1983), 109.
8. "More about Holy Poverty. Which Is Voluntary Poverty." *Catholic Worker,* February 1945, 1, 2, http://dorothyday.catholicworker.org/articles/150.html.
9. Ibid.
10. Dorothy Day, "Poverty and Pacifism," *Catholic Worker,* December 1944, 1, http://www.catholicworker.org/dodyday/reprint2.cfm?TextID=223.
11. Riegle, *Dorothy Day: Portraits,* 65.

12. See *On Pilgrimage*, May 1948, 75–92, http://www.catholic worker.org/dorothyday/Reprint2.cfm?TextID=480.

13. Dorothy Day, "Our Stand," *Catholic Worker*, June 1940, 1, 4, http://www.catholicworker.org/dorothyday/daytext.cfm ?TextID=360&SearchTerm=war.

14. Dorothy Day, "Pacifism," *Catholic Worker*, May 1936, 8, http://www.catholicworker.org/dorothyday/Reprint2.cfm?TextID=215.

15. Day, "Our Stand."

16. Charles Gallagher, "Our Brothers, the Jews," *America*, November 9, 2009, http://americamagazine.org/print/issue /714/article/our-brothers-jews.

17. Dorothy Day, "Our Country Passes from Undeclared War to Declared War; We Continue Our Christian Pacifist Stand," *Catholic Worker*, January 1942, 1, 4, http://www.catholic worker.org/dorothyday/Reprint2.cfm?TextID=868.

18. Dorothy Day, "We Go on Record: The CW Response to Hiroshima," *Catholic Worker* (September 1945): 1, http://www .catholicworker.org/dorothyday/daytext.cfm?TextID=554.

19. Ibid.

Chapter 6: Spreading a Gospel of Peace in the Age of Nuclear War

1. Editorial, *Catholic Worker*, November 1945.

2. "Who Then Is Our Brother?" *Catholic Worker*, December 1947, http://dorothyday.catholicworker.org/articles/156.html.

3. Dorothy Day, "Our Brothers, the Communists," in *Liberating Faith: Religious Voices for Justice, Peace, and Ecological Wisdom,* ed. Roger Gottlieb (Lanham, MD: Rowman & Littlefield, 2003), 251.

4. John Cooney, *The American Pope: The Life and Times of Francis Cardinal Spellman* (New York: New York Times Books, 1984), 191.

5. For more information on this strike, read David L. Gregory, "Dorothy Day, Workers' Rights and Catholic Authenticity," in *Fordham Urban Law Journal* 26, no. 5 (1998), http:// ir.lawnet.fordham.edu/ulj/vol26/iss5/2/.

6. Jean Howerton, "Ex-Red Editor, Now a Catholic, Call[s] U.S. 'Practically Marxist,'" *The Courier Journal*, March 5, 1949, 2.

7. As quoted by Gregory, "Dorothy Day, Workers' Rights, and Catholic Authenticity."

8. This story combines information gleaned from a phone interview with Jack Ford and a letter of invitation written by Sister George Marie Long of Ursuline College, dated January 5, 1952, Dorothy Day Archives, Marquette University.

9. "Father Loftus, Official at Bellarmine, Dies," *The Courier Journal*, January 8, 1969.

10. "Civil Defense Drill Protests: Dorothy Day and Friends Sit in for Peace," Marquette University, April 2009, http://www.marquette.edu/library/archives/News/spotlight/04-2009.shtml.

11. Joyce Hollyday, "The Dream that Has Endured: Clarence Jordan and Koinonia," *Sojourners* 8, no. 2 (December 1979), http://www.koinoniapartners.org/History/Dream.html.

12. "On Pilgrimage—May 1957," *Catholic Worker*, May 1957, 3, 6, http://www.catholicworker.org/dorothyday/Reprint2.cfm?TextID=722.

13. Ibid.

14. "The Case of Cardinal McIntyre," *Catholic Worker*, July–August 1964, 1, 6, 8, http://www.catholicworker.org/dorothyday/Reprint2.cfm?TextID=196.

15. Marifeli Pérez-Stable, *The Cuban Revolution: Origins, Course, and Legacy* (New York: Oxford University Press, 1993), 26.

16. Ibid., 30.

17. Dorothy Day, "About Cuba," *Catholic Worker*, July–August 1961, 1, 2, 7, 8, www.catholicworker.org.

18. Dorothy Day, "Pilgrimage to Cuba—Part I," *Catholic Worker*, September 1962, 1, 6, www.catholicworker.org.

19. Invitation sent from Virginia Naeve and Alice Pollard to Dorothy Day regarding "Women's Peace Pilgrimage to the Vatican." Dorothy Day Archives, Marquette University, D-5 Box 2.

20. "Report of Some of the Women," Dorothy Day Archives, Marquette University, D-5, Box 2.

21. Jim Forest, *All Is Grace: A Biography of Dorothy Day* (Maryknoll: Orbis Books, 2011), 234.
22. Anne Klejment and Nancy Roberts, "The Catholic Worker and the Vietnam War," in *American Catholic Pacifism*, 153.
23. Jim Forest, "Thomas Merton and Dorothy Day: A Special Friendship," (lecture, Bellarmine University, Louisville, KY, October 13, 2010), http://jimandnancyforest.com/2010/10/thomas-merton-and-dorothy-day-a-special-friendship/.
24. Dorothy Day, "Theophane Venard and Ho Chi Minh," *Catholic Worker*, May 1954, 1, 6, http://www.catholicworker.org/dorothyday/Reprint2.cfm?TextID=667.
25. Ibid.
26. Ibid.
27. I am indebted to social ethicist Miguel de la Torre for the term "prototype of Latin American liberation theology."
28. "We Are Un-American: We Are Catholics," *Catholic Worker*, April 1948, 2, http://www.catholicworker.org/dorothyday/Reprint2.cfm?TextID=466.
29. William D. Miller, *A Harsh and Dreadful Love: Dorothy Day and the Catholic Worker Movement* (New York: Liveright, 1973), 320–321.
30. As quoted by Klejment and Roberts, "The Catholic Worker and the Vietnam War," 167, n. 35.
31. Ibid., 162.
32. There were two bracero or guest worker programs made through bilateral agreements between the United States and Mexico; the first one was between 1917 and 1921.
33. Philip Martin, "Braceros: History, Compensation," *Rural Migration News* 12, no. 2 (April 2006), http://migration.ucdavis.edu/rmn/more.php?id=1112_0_4_0.
34. Forest, *All Is Grace*, 270.

Chapter 7: Looking at Things as a Woman

1. David Scott, book review of *The Moral Vision of Dorothy Day: A Feminist Perspective* by June O'Connor, http://www.david

scottwritings.com/oconnormoralvision.html. (See chap.4, n. 16.)

2. "March 1948," *On Pilgrimage,* 38–51, from Dorothy Day Library on the Web, http://www.catholicworker.org/dorothy day/Reprint2.cfm?TextID=478.

3. June O'Connor, *The Moral Vision of Dorothy Day: A Feminist Perspective* (New York: Crossroad, 1991), 39.

4. Janet K. Ruffing, ed., *Mysticism and Social Transformation* (Syracuse University Press, 2001), 6.

5. Dorothy Day, *House of Hospitality* (New York: Sheed and Ward, 1939), 97, http://www.catholicworker.org/dorothy day/daytext.cfm?TextID=3.

6. As quoted by David L. Gregory, "Dorothy Day, Workers' Rights and Catholic Authenticity," *Fordham Urban Law Journal* 26, no. 5 (1998): 1386–87, http://ir.lawnet.fordham .edu/ulj/vol26/iss5/2/.

7. Jim Forest, *All Is Grace: A Biography of Dorothy Day* (Maryknoll, NY: Orbis Books, 2011), 191.

8. Mary O'Driscoll, ed., *Catherine of Siena: Passion for the Truth, Compassion for Humanity* (New York: New City Press, 1993), 37.

9. Dorothy Day, *The Duty of Delight,* ed. Robert Ellsberg (Milwaukee, WI: Marquette University Press, 2008), 74.

10. Stephanie Paulsell, *Honoring the Body: Meditations on a Christian Practice* (San Francisco: Jossey Bass, 2002), 10.

11. Ibid., 12–13.

12. Carolyn Walker Bynum, *Jesus as Mother: Studies in the Spirituality of the High Middle Ages* (Berkeley: University of California Press, 1982), 115.

13. Julian of Norwich, *Showings,* trans. Edmund Colledge and James Walsh (New York: Paulist Press, 1978), 295.

14. Rosalie Riegle, *Dorothy Day: Portraits by Those Who Knew Her* (Maryknoll: Orbis Books, 2003), 23.

15. Ibid., 20.

16. Ibid., 22.

17. Bynum, *Jesus as Mother,* 230.

18. Mechthild of Magdeburg, *The Flowing Light of the Godhead*, in *Mystics, Visionaries and Prophets*, ed. Shawn Madigan (Minneapolis: Fortress Press, 1998), 139.

19. *The Duty of Delight*, 26.

20. Dorothy Day, *On Pilgrimage* (Grand Rapids, MI: Wm. B. Eerdmans, 1999), 138.

21. O'Connor, *The Moral Vision of Dorothy Day*, 41.

22. Forest, *All Is Grace*, 31.

23. Feminist theologian Rosemary Radford Ruether describes three traditions of feminist liberation (liberal, socialist, and radical feminism) and draws on all three of these streams to develop a contemporary integrative vision of feminism. See Ruether, *Sexism and God-talk* (Boston: Beacon Press, 1993; reprint of 1983 ed.), 223.

24. "On Pilgrimage," *Catholic Worker*, June 1971, 2, 5, 6, 8, http://www.catholicworker.org/dorothyday/Reprint2.cfm?TextID=510.

25. Lisa Sowle Cahill, *Sex, Gender, and Christian Ethics* (Cambridge University Press, 1996), 208.

26. Katherine M. Yohe, "Dorothy Day: Love for One's Daughter, Love for the Poor," *Horizons* 31/2 (2004): 273.

27. Dorothy Day, "Having a Baby," *New Masses*, June 1928, 6.

28. *The Duty of Delight*, 34.

29. Debra Campbell, "The Catholic Earth Mother: Dorothy Day and Women's Power in the Church," *Cross Currents* (Fall 1984): 280.

Chapter 8: A Personal Postscript: Dorothy Day's Legacy for Contemporary Christians

1. Dorothy Day, *Selected Writings*, 4th ed., Robert Ellsberg (Maryknoll, NY: Orbis Press, 2009), 102.

Index

abbess, 174–77, 186
Addams, Jane (1860–1935), 49, 98
agronomic universities, 66
   See also farming communes
air raid drills, 130, 133–34
   Catholic Worker protest, 134
   See also Hennacy, Ammon
America, xiv, 32, 114, 211n16
Aquinas, Thomas (1225–1274), 109
Astor, John Jacob (1763–1848), 35
Augustine of Hippo (354–430), 72–74, 82, 83, 108, 109
   Confessions 74, 82

Baptism, 25, 27, 28, 117, 162
   See also conditional baptism
Basil the Great (330–379), 57, 74
Batterham, Forster (1894–1984), 71,

81, 163, 184, 186, 206n36
   relationship with Day, 23–29
Bellarmine College, ix–x, 129, 131–32, 212n9, 213n23
Benedict, 147, 193
Benedictine, 66, 68
Berdyaev, Nikolai (1874–1948), 40
Bernard of Clairvaux (1090–1153), 174–76, 178
Berrigan
   Daniel, xv, 49, 123, 147, 150, 152
   Philip (1923–2002), xv, 123, 147, 150
Bethune, Ade (1914–2002), xv, 50–51
Bible
   Psalms, 16, 67, 193, 194
   Matthew (6:31), 104; (6:33), 104; (25:31–46), 36; genealogy, 24; Gospel of, 100. *See also*

Sermon on the Mount
   Acts (2:43), 38
   Romans (12:4–5), 62
   First Corinthians (12:14), 68
Bracero Program, 155–56; 213nn32, 33
Burroughs, Nannie Helen (1879–1961), 49

Canonization, xv, 89
capitalism, 26, 37, 40, 42, 46, 64, 72, 94–95, 125
Carnegie, Andrew (1835–1919), 35
Castro, Fidel, 139, 141
Catherine of Siena (1347–1380), 72, 83–84, 167, 171–72, 214n8
Catholic Worker, xiv, xvii, 88, 101, 110, 114, 115, 117, 118, 122, 124, 125, 129, 134, 140, 145, 146, 147, 150, 152, 154, 170,

Index

Index

Index

CPSIA information can be obtained at www.ICGtesting.com
Printed in the USA
BVOW03s0152231014

371952BV00012B/145/P